Biography and Sermons

of

MARSHALL KEEBLE, *Evangelist*

Edited by

B. C. GOODPASTURE

GOSPEL ADVOCATE COMPANY
Nashville, Tennessee

Published by Gospel Advocate Co.
P.O. Box 150
Nashville, TN 37202
www.gospeladvocate.com

First Published: 1931

ISBN 0-89225-502-1

PREFACE

For several years there has been a growing demand, among both colored and white churches, for a volume of Keeble's sermons. It has been the judgment of all that these sermons should be preserved in the vernacular in which they were delivered, otherwise they would not be Keeble's at all. To this end the services of an expert court reporter, Miss Connie Alderman, of Valdosta, Georgia, were secured. She was instructed to take these sermons *exactly* as delivered. She succeeeded so well that the transcript of her notes required but few minor corrections. Brother Keeble went over all these sermons carefully. They are *his*. The Charts that accompany them are exact reproductions of the originals. These sermons were delivered in Valdosta, Georgia, July 20-24, 1931.

At first it was the purpose of the editor to prepare a much larger number of sermons for this work; but on maturer consideration it seemed best to issue a small volume now, and perhaps another later. In view of the present "depression," a larger volume would possibly be too expensive for some who would want it. It must be borne in mind that this book has been prepared primarily for our colored brethren.

This volume is sent forth with the prayer that it may be instrumental in turning many to righteousness.   B. C. G.

CONTENTS

ILLUSTRATIONS

—

BROTHER KEEBLE

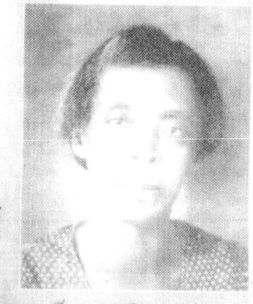

SISTER KEEBLE

CHAPTER I.

MARSHALL KEEBLE.

The subject of this sketch was born on a farm near Murfreesboro, in Rutherford County, Tennessee, on the 7th of December, 1878. When he was four years of age his parents, Robert and Mittie Keeble, moved to Nashville, Tennessee. Years later his father died in Nashville; but he, his wife and two children, as well as his aged mother, still live there.

He attended the Bell View and Noles Schools of Nashville; but never went beyond the seventh grade. Although limited in education, as we think of it in terms of school attendance, he has, nevertheless, acquired a remarkable knowledge of the Bible and human nature. He knows how to reach and move the hearts of men. His audiences grow. They never seem to tire of hearing him. His preaching is not "with enticing words of man's wisdom, but in demonstration of the Spirit and of power." It was his good fortune, at the age of nineteen, to be married to Minnie, daughter of S. W. Womack, and a graduate of Fisk University. She has helped him much in his studies and in his efforts as a preacher. From his father-in-law, who was a preacher of great humility, meekness, and faith, he learned many of the basic principles of the Christian life; from Alexander Campbell, another colored preacher of the church of Christ, he learned many things that have contributed to his success as a preacher of the gospel. Besides, he has diligently studied the writings of many of the white brethren, mentioning in particular those of David Lipscomb, T. B. Larimore, N. B. Hardeman, and H. Leo Boles. He has burned much midnight oil.

The first sermon he preached was in Nashville, Tennessee, nearly twenty-nine years ago. At this time he had been a member of the church about ten years, having been baptized by Preston Taylor in his fourteenth year. His mother-in-law, Sallie Womack, who continues to rejoice in his success, did much to encourage him to study the Bible and preach. He frequently went with Alexander Campbell on his preaching tours to assist him in his meetings and to be taught by him. As a result he soon learned to appear before large audiences and developed into a preacher. During the past sixteen years he has been in the field, doing what is commonly called evangelistic work. The early years of this period were years of great self-denial and suffering. His support was pitifully small. Using his own words, "I suffered much, but wife never once complained of the suffering we were going through. Had she complained, I could not have succeeded. We kept all our sufferings to ourselves, and we never murmured. I believe she deserves more praise for what little I have done than I do." After he had spent a number of trying years in evangelistic work, Brother A. M. Burton became greatly interested in his work, and sent him to many places at his own expense. Brother Keeble feels that if it had not been for this assistance he could not have carried on his work. He is unable to find words with which to express his appreciation of Brother Burton's interest and support. Following the example of Brother Burton, others became interested in his work, and now white churches from all over the country are calling and supporting him in meetings among his people. He is ever grateful for the great missionary spirit being mani-

tested by his white brethren in sending him to his own
race.

The first meeting he held in which there was a large
number of additions was in Henderson, Tennessee.
There were sixty-nine baptisms. At Tampa, Florida,
in 1927, he conducted a tent meeting which resulted in
ninety-nine baptisms. In 1929, he baptized ninety-two
in the St. Petersburg (Florida) meeting. Eighty-six
were baptized in the Fort Smith (Arkansas) meeting;
sixty-five, at Lakeland, Florida; fifty-eight at Jackson,
Tennessee; one hundred and sixty-three in the first, and
one hundred and sixty-six in the second, Valdosta
(Georgia) meeting. As this goes to press he closes a
successful meeting here in Atlanta with one hundred and
sixty-six additions. The white churches in the respective
cities, have sponsored all these meetings. All told,
Marshall Keeble has baptized about six thousand people.
Among these are numbered one hundred and eighty-
three preachers, and his own mother, whom he baptized
about five years ago. He has also been responsible for
the conversion of about one thousand white people who
have attended his meetings from time to time. He has
held a number of debates; in several of these he has
baptized his opponent before the time allotted for the
debate was over. As a result of his labors forty-eight
congregations have been established.

He has preached in the following States: Alabama,
Arkansas, Tennessee, Texas, Georgia, California, Mis-
sissippi, Florida, Michigan, West Virginia, South Caro-
lina, Illinois, Missouri, Indiana, Oklahoma, Kentucky,
and also the District of Columbia.

BROTHER KEEBLE AS A PREACHER.

Nature has done much for Marshall Keeble. He has
been blessed with a strong mind in a strong body. He

preaches almost daily, month after month and year after year, going from the Great Lakes to the Gulf and from the Capital City to the Golden Gate; and yet no one ever hears him complain of being sick or tired. He preaches in houses, in tents, and in the wide outdoors; he preaches to families, to small gatherings, and to thousands; and yet always and everywhere he seems to be in fine physical condition and in the enjoyment of an abiding freshness and activity of mind. His keen logic, his unstudied and apt illustration, his irresistible flow of humor, his ability quickly to grasp and handle unexpected situations, and his knowledge of the Bible —these all give evidence of the alertness and vigor of his mind.

But perhaps the secret of his power and success is to be found in his humble and prayerful walk with God. He believes that "they that wait upon the Lord shall renew their strength." In his preaching one sees reflected the devotional spirit of the Psalmist, the glowing fire of the prophets, the evangelistic fervor and zeal of the apostles, and the fearless courage of Him who cleansed the temple. He impresses the listener as one who is mightily in earnest. He seems to feel that woe is unto him if he preaches not the gospel. His mission is to preach Christ and save souls. His heart yearns for the salvation of his people. He is not made proud and boastful by his success and the many complimentary things the white brethren say to him, but rather made the more humble and the more grateful to an All-wise Father for enabling him to be used for good. He realizes that if he should cease to be meek and humble he would be bereft of his strength as Samson was when he was shorn of his hair. With him, "the power is in the gospel, not in Keeble."

As a fair example of Brother Keeble's work, we submit an account of his meetings in Valdosta, Ga. This article, written by Brother A. B. Lipscomb, appeared recently in the Christian Leader, and is here used with his permission. It is an accurate and graphic description of Keeble in action. It is as follows:

"The second meeting among the Negroes of Valdosta, Ga., conducted by the colored evangelist, Marshall Keeble, of Nashville, Tenn., came to a close on August 9, 1931. All told, one hundred and sixty-six persons were baptized, chiefly adults. This was three more than the number baptized in the first meeting, just about one year before. Between the two meetings one hundred and twenty persons were baptized under the teaching, preaching, and faithful leadership of Brother Luke Miller, who was left in charge of the work. 'I picked up those whom Brother Keeble crippled,' is how Miller modestly describes his labors. Thus we note that within the short space of one year's time, in a community where no congregation of colored disciples existed, one has been established with a membership of more than four hundred souls. Through the help of the white brethren a large, commodious house of worship has been secured and regular worship prevails. Their sick and unemployed members are being looked after and much constructive work is being accomplished. The white brethren made the down payment on the house, but, to encourage their colored brothers in lessons of frugality and self-sacrifice, the remaining payments are being met through the medium of the regular Lord's-day contributions.

"To what shall we attribute this remarkable success? How explain results which, had they been accomplished under the preaching of a white evangelist, would have been heralded far and wide? In what sense is Keeble a 'big preacher,' if in any sense at all? The answer, I believe, is suggested by his own statement: 'It's not Keeble, but the Bible is right.' If you have heard him preach, then you are quite familiar with the slogan. For not a sermon is preached but what he does not sound it out again and again. The secret of success lies in the fact that Keeble is just big and brave and humble and smart enough to magnify God's word in almost every sentence he utters. It is a simple thought; there is nothing original about it; it is as old as the Bible itself; something that was proclaimed by Moses and the prophets, featured by Christ and the apostles, and revived by the leaders of the Restoration Movement— and yet this colored man proclaims it in the vernacular of his own race with truly telling effect, and with all the freshness and beauty of a new slogan. All his listeners are visibly impressed with the strength of his statement. The older colored sisters, sitting in the same corner of the big tent, shake their heads gravely and repeat after him in reverent monotone: 'Dat's it, the Bible is right.' Scores of white people, standing on the outside or sitting in their cars, more decorously nod their approval. Nearly everybody gets the impression that this colored preacher, a self-made man, with but little literary education, but with one great Book in his hand, is standing on a solid rock from which all this world's wiseacres can never make him budge! There is in his straightforward, earnest speech not merely the reminder, but the positive conviction of both prophet and apostle: 'The grass withereth, the flower fadeth: but the word of our God shall stand forever.' If anybody cherishes the maudlin sentiment that the Twentieth Century has outgrown the New Testament and that its simple conditions of salvation have become too trite and commonplace to be any longer interesting to the public, I recommend that he sit through a Keeble meeting. In the meetings here at Valdosta he quoted Acts 2: 38 so frequently and made its meaning so plain that now little children, both white and black, have it at their tongues' end, and are actually using it to confound some of their elders who did not hear the sermons.

"The work among the Negroes was sponsored and financed by the white disciples. We have never made a better investment for the Lord, nor one that brought such quick and happy results. Brother Keeble unhesitatingly says that, without this moral and financial support, he could have done little or nothing. We have tried all the way through to keep ourselves in the background, to help where help was needed; but let the colored brethren conduct their own meeting in their own way, in the realization that Keeble knows his own race better than we do. And this undoubtedly is the wisest course to pursue when planning a meeting for them. Not only have hundreds of souls been converted to Christ; but as a further result of the meetings a new citizenry has been created among our Negro population. We have better workmen, better porters, better farm hands, better cooks, better nurses, better housemaids. Verily it pays to preach the gospel to them and teach them how to think and work in terms of the grand old Book.

"Racial differences and the question of social equality were not discussed during the meetings. There was no occasion for it. But the duty of Christian brotherhood has been recognized and practiced to the fullest extent. In that respect we have kept Paul's words before us: 'There is neither Jew nor Greek, there is neither bond nor free, there is neither male nor female: for ye are all one in Christ Jesus.' What has been done in Valdosta may be done in countless other home fields where the Negroes flourish and need to be taught. Is it not fitting that the members of the race that our fathers kept in the bondage of slavery, but to whom civilization brought the gift of emancipation, should now be led by the white children of the present generation out of the darkness and bondage of sin into 'the glorious liberty of the children of God?' Verily a harvest is waiting at our very doors."

COMMENDATORY.

Brother Keeble's manner of life and work has been such that he enjoys the confidence and esteem of the white, as well as the colored, brethren everywhere. His meekness, his Christlike humility, his unstinted willingness to be used of the Lord in His service, his unwavering faith in, and loyalty to, the Sacred Volume—these are all highly appreciated and commended. It is likely that this volume will fall into the hands of those unacquainted with Brother Keeble and his great work; and for the benefit of this class in particular and for the gratification of all in general a few of the many fine things that have been said concerning him and his work are here quoted.

Brother Hall Laurie Calhoun, Minister of the Belmont Ave. Church of Christ, Nashville, Tenn., says: "I take pleasure in saying that I know Brother Keeble quite well. I heard him preach daily for a whole week. His sermons are scriptural, logical, and well calculated to bring people to Christ. I am sure that the book of sermons just appearing coming from him will be well worth the price which it costs and much more to the people who buy the book and read it."

Brother A. M. Burton, President of the Life and Casualty Insurance Co., of Nashville, Tenn., writes: "It is a very great pleasure to me to say a good word in behalf of Bro. Marshall Keeble. During the past ten or fifteen years that it has been my privilege to recommend him to our white brethren for his work's sake he has made good as a preacher of the gospel. In my opinion, his humility, his prayerful life, and his fearlessness in proclaiming the truths of the Bible are responsible for the great good that he has done. I feel that his book of sermons will carry much of that same convicting and convincing power that has been characteristic of him in the pulpit."

Prof. H. Leo Boles, President of David Lipscomb College, Nashville, Tenn., says: "Brother M. Keeble knows the plan of salvation and the duties of a Christian life better than any other preacher among our colored brethren. He is true to the teachings of the Bible and is loyal to the church of our Lord. I would commend his sermons to any one as being sound in gospel truth and simple in expression."

From Prof. N. B. Hardeman, President of Freed-Hardeman College, comes this enthusiastic expression: "I have known Bro. M. Keeble since 1922, and have followed him with interest and appreciation all along the years since. I have said many times, privately and publicly, that I consider Bro. Keeble one of the very best preachers in the church of Christ, and that he is possibly doing more good than any other man among us. I have baptized a number of white people who were really converted under the preaching of Bro. Keeble. His simplicity and humility, plus his ability to tell the story, mean much to the cause of Christ. I believe a book of his sermons in his characteristic way will prove interesting and helpful."

Many other such expressions could be given, but these are sufficient to indicate the high esteem in which Brother Keeble is justly held. It is our hope and prayer that he may be spared many more years in which to carry the glorious gospel to his neglected race.

B. C. G.

POWER OF THE WRITTEN WORD.

———

1. When buying house get W. Deed.

2. When paying debt get W. Re.

3. Be sure to have your Deed Re.

4. Check no good without N.

(This above refers to every day Business.)

Have you obeyed the written Word of God?

(This last part refers to all who desire to please our
    God.)

CHAPTER II.

"THE POWER OF THE WRITTEN WORD."

My Beloved friends, Brethren and Sisters, it is quite a privilege, quite a blessing to have this opportunity to stand in front of such an intelligent audience at this time. We appreciate your presence and we are thankful for the interest that is being manifested in the very beginning of this meeting, and I hope, I pray that when the invitation is extended and the privilege granted, there will be some precious soul ready to respond to the invitation. This meeting is for the express purpose of enlightening and developing our minds to that spiritual sense and that spiritual knowledge of what God wants us to become, to become His children.

On last night we were blessed with a splendid meeting and several confessions. The beginning of the meeting, I think, is very encouraging. The very first day there were five confessions and two of them were baptized this morning and three last night. We hope that there will be responses in every service we have, and we pray that many of you will have a sufficient amount of courage and boldness to come to the knowledge of the truth—come to Jesus as the Bible directs. I see no need of us being afraid to surrender to what the teaching of the Bible is: and for that reason, this meeting is, and is in progress for the development of our minds upon these religious subjects that we shall discuss night after night.

I want to further say that I am sure you are somewhat curious to know why Brother Goodpasture, who sits to my left, and those intelligent ladies that sit with him, you are wondering no doubt what is that for. I shall remove your curiosity by making a statement informing you of their purpose at this time. Brother Goodpasture has been, and is, one of the best friends that I have and not only that, I don't know of a man that is any more greatly interested in the work I am attempting to do daily, and for that reason, he has suggested that a number of sermons at some proper place be taken down to be put in print, so that they could be put in book form and, in that way, thousands of people possibly would get the benefit of the lessons that I would never see and for that reason he has put himself to some trouble to prove his interest. He has employed this splendid lady, who is able to take down these lessons and prepare them for the public and hand them down to us in print; so that all of us, and people that I shall never see, will be benefited. So that explains that; and I hope that you can understand now why it is that they are here. And then another thing. I have lots of white friends that I told you about frequently when I was here last year, and they have all done everything they could to encourage me in the work; and I know, and you know, that I could not have such friends and such encouragement if I were not a man that was living so they could befriend me. They couldn't befriend me if I were living a dirty, filthy life, and I wouldn't have either colored or white friends if I didn't live as the Bible teaches, and in that way I have got friends by the hundreds. I hope to be able to live in such a way as to retain their friendship, and to be worthy of the friends I now have; and may be able to make many more.

Now then, the subject this evening is "The Power of the Written Word." One reason why we appreciate this subject in the beginning of the meeting is because of the fact that the average man and the average woman have been taught that the Bible of itself, the written word, is not sufficient; that there must be miraculous outpourings of the Holy Spirit, some miraculous happenings in their conversion that they cannot understand. Then they claim that it is the working of the Holy Ghost independent of God's word. I am one of those that believe that all the power is in the word of God and if you ever get any power to do anything for Christ, it must come through the written word. In the 20th chapter, Book of St. John, in the latter part of that chapter, John said, "And many other signs truly did Jesus in the presence of His disciples, which are not written in this book: But these are written, that ye might believe that Jesus is the Christ, the Son of God; and that believing ye might have life through His name." It is the written word, and to prove to you that I am right on that point, there is not a man living today that knows anything about God's will, except what he learned from the written word. There is not a man living today that knows anything about heaven except what he learned from the written word. We wouldn't know that Shadrach, Meshach, and Abednego was in the fiery furnace if it wasn't written; we wouldn't know that God created the heaven and the earth, and the earth was without form, and void, and the Spirit of God moved upon the waters—we wouldn't know any of these at all if it wasn't written. And friends, we wouldn't know that such a character ever made footprints upon the earth as Jesus Christ if it had not been written; we wouldn't have known that He died upon the Cross of Calvary if it hadn't been written, and the supreme thing is, we wouldn't know that He was raised from the dead if the Bible hadn't said so. That same Bible tells us how to become God's children. You can't get around it, no way to get around it. Why the people of this town, especially preachers, are extremely excited over this meeting, and that is for the reason that Brother Keeble is attempting to call his people back to the Bible, to do away with the disciplines, manuals and creeds from the people and back to the written word of God.

Now we want to call your attention to some things of a material nature, things that happen in our everyday life, and after we review those things I am going to call your attention briefly to things that pertain to our salvation.

The first thing I want to suggest is, if you were buying a house, would you not have a written contract? How many men in this audience would buy a piece of property, it matters not how much it cost, were it not in writing? Would you do that? Not a man would do that. You wouldn't invest fifteen cents in a piece of property without having it in writing; if not, it is possible that the whole of your fifteen cents is thrown away. I remember a man in my city, Nashville, Tennessee, who bought a piece of property once from a man that was a good friend of his. The man told him, "You don't need a written deed, I will treat you right, John." And he would, he was just and good, and thought lots of John and John took him at his word, not thinking the man would die and leave him with a piece of property he had paid for; but he did die and poor John lost his property because he had nothing in writing. The point I want to make is, when you stand at the bar of judgment after you have been slaving for a number of years and yet have no deed—got no eternal home. What was the matter? No written contract—went around guessing and feeling your way to heaven. Got to get your written contract. I want a contract that is stamped in the blood of Christ. Don't go before God with a contract unstamped.

There is another important feature of a material nature and that is, when paying a debt, you get a receipt. Now I don't have to tell you what you are supposed to have intelligence enough to know, and that is, get a receipt, but I want to make a point—is the reason I tell you. I know you know better than that, but if you don't, better be careful and get your receipt. Now friends, listen, I remember once in Florence, Alabama, there was a lady when I was there the last time that left twenty-five cents to pay her insurance agent, and the little child paid the agent but forgot to get a receipt for the twenty-five cents as she couldn't find her book. When the agent came back, he came back—naturally he was honest—expecting the same twenty-five cents because he hadn't registered it on his book and never gave a receipt for it, not meaning any harm and not trying to steal. If the lady had had that in writing, she might have gotten her twenty-five cents back, but she didn't have it and the little child was too little to talk up to the man and of course, the quarter got away. Well now friends, I want to say that in everything you do, especially in paying debts, get a receipt. I remember once my wife owed a debt; we bought some furniture, and we were paying for it as colored people generally do, on the installment plan. And now then, while we were paying for this furniture on the installment plan, I was sending the money—I was away from home all the time—and I was sending her the money to pay the man, and she was. So when I came home one

O. L. Aker, Minister
Florence, Ala.

John Vaughner, Minister
St. Petersburg, Fla.

Luke Miller, Minister
Valdosta, Ga.

Percy Ricks, Minister
Tuscumbia, Ala.

Jas. F. Hewin, Minister
Birmingham, Ala.

Thomas Dickson, Minister
Huntsville, Ala.

FELLOW WORKERS

These are men whom Brother Keeble has either baptized or encouraged
to preach. They render him great service in his meetings. They preach
for the churches with which they worship.

time to spend a day or two, she said "Let's go down and pay our last installment on the furniture," and I said, "All right." She said, "We don't owe but one more payment," and that sounded good to me. I went down town with her and she walked into the furniture company and slammed down the money to pay the last payment and the bookkeeper tells her, "You owe just one more payment." I looked kinder frightened—didn't sound good to me. I looked at her and at him. He told her positively, "You owe me one more installment," and she just as positively insisted, "I don't." I scratched my head. And he said, "That's the way it is on the book, Minnie," and she said, "I don't care what is on the book, I have paid everything but the last payment I am paying now." And he said, "Well, that is the way it stands on the books and I can't give you credit for it." She said, "Well, I can get your receipt." "Well, bring it in and it will be perfectly all right, bring in the receipt proving it and we'll check on the receipt." We got on the electric car to go home, and when we got on the car, I said, "You sure you got it?" And it kinder fretted her for me to believe—and I was kinder afraid—she didn't. I asked her, "Are you sure you have it?" She said, "I have got it at home." We went home and she pulled off her hat and her coat and she went to work looking in every old kind of a sack she had, and I don't know what kind of books she did pull out looking for the receipt—looked through so many things we had about decided she didn't have it, when she called out, "Honey, here it is," and I said, "Thank God." So when we found the receipt she said, "Let's go back right now," and we went back on the car right away, right on back to town, didn't wait until tomorrow. We went right in the store and presented all the receipts. The bookkeeper checked up on it and said, "That's right, Minnie, it's all paid. I don't see why it wasn't registered on the book." The proprietor of the big concern said, "Minnie, anything you want come and get it, it was just a little mistake of the bookkeeper." But what was the truth? Minnie had kept the receipts. Above everything, keep your receipts. If you are going to heaven and you appear before Jesus Christ at the final consummation of all things and at the judgment seat of Christ where all nations must appear and you stand there and you haven't got a receipt written by Jesus Christ, signed with His blood, you will have to check off with your debt unpaid. You are going to have to walk up there with a receipt. Don't you go fooling around without a receipt. You have got to get a receipt. Have to get your receipt, that is all there is about it.

Now then, may I call your attention to another fact? In buying property you get a deed and have the deed recorded. That is another important feature about these material matters. You all know before I come to it, that I have a point I am driving at. Now then listen please, if I tell you that I own this property, the property this tent is erected on, nobody has a right to dispute it, nobody knows anything about my business. I can say what I want to. I can say that piece of property was mine and some of you, gentlemen, would think kinder suspicious about it and you would go around to one another and say, "I don't believe he owns it, but before I call him a liar, I believe I'll go to the courthouse and look over the records," and you go up there and find nothing on record that belongs to Brother Keeble. You come back and say, "Brother Keeble, we didn't think you would tell us a lie that way before the public." What would I say? "Well, brethren, I didn't

know you were going that far with it. I didn't know
you were going to investigate." Brethren, we are living
in an age of investigation, nothing that won't stand investigation won't pass. That is true of a piece of property I might say I owned; and the same thing would be
true of the church I am a member of, if it were not
mentioned in the written—recorded—word of God. 1
would suggest that you go to the record and see if you
can find your church on record, and if your church is not
on record, you did the same thing about the church that
I did about the property.

Now then, gentlemen, if your church is not on record,
I wouldn't be in nothing—I am honest, friends, I am
sincere, and I wouldn't be in nothing that couldn't be
found on record. Be baptized and get into the church
that we read about in God's written word.

And now then, I call your attention to another feature
of a material nature, and this is important. Guess you
all know this too. A check is no good without a name.
Guess everybody here knows that. And in these hard
times of depression, not much good with a name. Listen
friends, a check is no good, no good without a name.
I can remember an incident I once read of an Evangelist
that was conducting a meeting in a certain city and
there was a lady in the audience who heard him every
night preach that there was nothing in a name, that the
name hasn't a thing to do with it; tells the membership
to continue and go ahead and work out your salvation,
the name don't mean anything. Where did he get that?
And one night this lady said to him, "Look here, I want
to help you and have some part with you in your evangelistic work. I want you to come to my residence tomorrow. I want to give you a contribution." Well, I
need not tell you that all preachers love to hear some-

thing like that; and whether or not he was down there early next morning, it is not necessary to say. Just as early as he could get there, he was knocking on the door—knocked on the door and the lady responded and came to the door and asked him to have a seat on the front porch; and she went in the house and wrote him a check. He politely thanked her, put on his hat and went down the street. Went to the First National Bank, pushed the check under the Cashier's window. The Cashier looked at the check and passed it back to him. Then he got interested in what was the matter with the check. The Cashier said, "No name signed to it," and he said, "Oh, she forgot to sign it," and he went back to the lady's house to inform her that she had forgotten to sign it. He calls her attention to the fact; and the lady says, "No, I never forgot to sign it, you preached and have been preaching several nights that there was nothing in a name and I just didn't put one on there, thought there was nothing in it." Now friends, that man got caught in his own net. Oh! she was nice enough to put her name on it then and let him go to the bank and get the money on the check, but she told him this: "Don't you never preach that no more." And I don't guess he ever did. Common sense will tell you there is something in a name. If there wasn't something in a name you would get lost in this town. If these streets wasn't named you couldn't go over this town, you would get lost. You would have to have a name on these streets and then you can tell a party where a man lives at and where you can find him. Then you have to know the name of the man you are looking for. Could you go on the street and tell somebody, "I am looking for a man on this street, I don't know the man's name. Oh, there's nothing in a name, where

is he at?" Now you stop that foolishness, there is something in a name; for in the 4th chapter of the Book of
Acts, verse 12, friends, it says, "There is none other
name under heaven given among men, whereby we must
be saved." You can get some one else's if you want to,
but there is none other name under heaven by which
you can be saved. Might as well quit your foolishness.
Get down to business, gentlemen, and find the name that
you are walking around here looking for. If I wear
the name Mormon, I represent the Mormons; if I wear
the name Russellite, I represent Russell and not Jesus
Christ. It is as plain as can be. All right, there is something in a name, gentlemen, and I never intend to go
up to my Master representing something that is not in
the written word of God. I want to go there with a
name I can find on the pages of the Book of Inspiration.
In Matthew 16th chapter, 13th verse, when Jesus came
to the coasts of Cæsarea Philippi, he propounded a question to his disciples and said, "Whom do men say that I
the Son of man am?" That is, what are the people saying about me around Cæsarea? and they said, "Some
say that thou art John the Baptist, and others that thou
art Jeremiah, and then another crowd that says thou art
Elias," and they were all divided. Ought he just have
a͏͏ epted any of these? If there is nothing in a name,
ny one of them would have been all right. But did he
do it? No, Sir. He saith unto them, "But whom say ye
that I am?" You have seen me feed thousands with the
five loaves and the fishes, you have seen me unstop
the deaf ear and open the blind eye. You were there
when I raised Lazarus from the dead. "Whom say ye
that I am?" Peter said, "Thou art the Christ, the Son
of the living God," and when he heard this he said,
"Blessed art thou, Simon Barjona, for flesh and blood

hath not revealed it unto thee, but my Father which is in heaven, and upon this rock I will build my church, and the gates of hell shall not prevail against it." What is the matter you all don't like it when I say "Upon this rock I will build the Baptist Church?" Listen at that grumbling! "Upon this rock I will build the Methodist Church." Now listen at that. I will get something that suits you. Upon this rock I will build "my" church, and the gates of hell shall not prevail. Somebody wants to ask whose church is "my" church. He didn't say Christ's Church or Church of Christ. No, not in so many words, but that's what he meant. When I say "my" handkerchief, I mean Keeble's handkerchief or the handkerchief of Keeble. If you know "my" about that handkerchief, why is it you don't know "my" about the church?

Now then, gentlemen, there is power in the written word, not only in spiritual matters but there is power in the written word in material business of today. No material business of today can be considered legitimate until you get it in writing. If you go to buy anything you must sign a contract. When I went to buy that furniture, I signed one and then he asked my wife to sign it. Both of us had to sign it so neither one can dodge it. That is the idea. He said, "Sign on the dotted line," and I signed. "There is another dotted line, where is your wife?" So, my friends, nothing is legitimate unless you have it in writing and a man is not considered a good business man in his business without writing, and so it is in religion—we must have a contract signed in the blood of Jesus Christ.

Just a few thoughts and I am through. You say, Brother Keeble you are right on the buying of a house, get a written contract, that's right. When paying a

debt, get a written receipt. When you get a deed, have
it recorded. Check no good without a name, you acknowledge that. How come you can see all of that and
you can't see this [pointing to question]? *"Have you
obeyed the written word?"* Have you become a Christian? Did you obey the written word? Did you go off
somewhere to church and claim you heard Christ say,
"Your sins are forgiven and soul set free?" A good
many told that. Why do you tell that? It is not written
in the Bible. It is not written since Jesus Christ shed
his blood on Calvary, came out of the grave as the con-
quering Christ. You can't find such a statement in the
New Testament since His blood was shed on Calvary.
I know you don't like to hear this. One lady at Fort
Smith, Arkansas, who used to come with her husband
to the meeting every night would go home fussing. She
and her husband were Baptists; they were good people,
morally good people, and they would come every night.
The wife would go back home mouthing about the sermon to her husband, because I was reading the Bible
like it was written. And he said, "Why don't you jot
down what the man says and find out if it is in the
Bible?" She said, "Already got it down, checking up
on him every night." The man couldn't read, so he said,
"Take the Bible and read it to me," and so she got the
Bible and began running over it. He drew up close to
get her to read it to him, and finally he said, "You found
anything?" A long time had expired, long enough for
anybody to find most anything, and she said, "Yes,
my God, here is all of it here." And then what happened? The next night that man and wife made the
confession, both of them were baptized into the church
that is written of in the New Testament; the church
hat the written word talks about. I wouldnit take no

chances and I wouldn't risk my soul in nothing that I couldn't find written on the pages of inspiration. Obeying the written word is the question that confronts us. What does it take to become a Christian; what does it mean to become a Christian? I tell you what to do when you go home tonight, you read the Second Chapter of the Book of Acts, just take the second chapter of Acts; you might read the 38th verse and you will see what the Apostles told the sinner to do in order to get his sins removed. Peter stood on the day of Pentecost and preached the first gospel sermon that was ever preached after Christ's blood was shed on Calvary; the first sermon that was ever preached after Christ conquered death, hell and the grave. Christ said, "Go ye into all the world and preach the gospel to every creature. He that believeth and is baptized shall be saved." (Mark 16: 15, 16.)

And now, gentlemen, here is what you have got to do. Peter told the three thousand on the day of Pentecost, when they asked him the question "Men and brethren, what shall we do?" Peter said "Repent, and be baptized every one of you in the name of Jesus Christ for the remission of sins and you shall receive the gift of the Holy Ghost." (Acts 2: 38.) It is written in everybody's Bible in this town; it is written in every Bible on every pulpit in every church in this town. The only way to get pardon for remission of sin is to get pardon through the blood of Christ. I was discussing this proposition with a gentleman at Hopkinsville, Ky., just before I came down here and he referred to the thief on the cross and attempted to show by the thief on the cross that we could be saved without being baptized; and of course, he couldn't prove it by that. But I let him have the benefit of the doubt and granted that the thief was

saved. You can't be saved like him, because he was
saved before Christ's blood was shed and he was saved
before Christ conquered death, hell and the grave; he
died under the law of Moses; he is now lying somewhere sleeping waiting on the "risurrection." When
Christ went back to heaven he went back by himself, never carried the thief, went back by himself. Once while I was preaching at Center Point,
Arkansas, an old lady came to me and said "Brother
Keeble, it's the blood of Christ that cleanses us from
all sins." I said "Yes, ma'am, it is the blood of Christ,
but where do you reach the blood?" She couldn't tell
to save her life. A lot of people claim that the blood
of Christ cleanses all sin. Get down to business, can
you tell where the blood is? If you want to know
where the blood is, the cleansing blood, go to the 19th
chapter of St. John, 34th verse, Jesus Christ hanging
on the cross of Calvary, after both thieves' legs were
broken, Jesus Christ was pierced in the side in his
death and forthwith came out blood and water. He
was dead, the Bible says, already dead. He was pierced
in the side and forthwith came out blood and water.
Water and blood came out of the wound together and
they are together tonight. Apostle Paul says in Romans
6: 4, "We are buried with him by baptism into death."
Friends, when you get ready to dye a garment, how do
you go about it? You grab the garment and souse it
in the water. What is that for? To reach the dye.
Where is the dye? In the water. Do any of you take
a package of dye and lay it on the garment and expect
it to be dyed? Friends, listen, you put that dye in the
water and it dissolves, then you baptize the garment
and bring the garment out stained with the dye. When
you baptize a man, he is stained with the blood of Jesus

Christ and comes out clean. Clean with the blood of
Christ. You can't get around that. We thought you
said it was the water. Tell you one thing, I will prove
by the Apostles, I believe it was Peter, in the 3rd chapter of the First Epistle of Peter, in the latter part of
the chapter, said "When once the long suffering of God
waited in the days of Noah, while the ark was preparing, wherein few, that is, eight souls were saved by
water. The like figure whereunto even baptism doth
also now save us." He said baptism did it; I don't
know anything about it, except what it says.

Now another thing; if you can find on the pages of
inspiration, where anybody can get religion, bring it in
to Brother Keeble and he will thank you for it. Go
read your Bible, it's not there, you can't get religion to
save your life. You can't find it. Not a man in Valdosta
got religion. If you can find it, bring it in and say,
"Brother Keeble, stop preaching like you do, we have
found it." If you can find it, bring it in and I'm gone.
Now you go to these preachers that have been telling
you to get religion; tell them to come down to the
point and show you where this is at in God's word.
Go to any of them tomorrow and ask him where the
passage is at and he will tell you, "You stay away from
that tent." Well now friends, don't you know that,
when you go to ask him where to find that passage that
says get religion and he tells you to stay away from
that tent, it is because you will find he has been falsely
teaching you?

May God help you come to Christ, he said "Come
unto me, all ye that labour and are heavy laden, and I
will give you rest. For my yoke is easy and my burden is light." He said "Behold, I stand at the door and
knock." I wonder isn't there somebody present willing

to let Jesus come into his heart? Are there any of you willing to bow in submission to His word? Will you not come and accept him tonight, while we stand together and sing?

BEEN TO WORSHIP, BUT WRONG.

Went a long ways.

Busy reading.

Philip began at the same S.

Preached unto him Jesus.

Here is Water.

Confess.

Baptized.

Rejoicing.

CHAPTER III.

BEEN TO WORSHIP, BUT WRONG.

We thank God that we are once more permitted to assemble together in the name of Jesus Christ for the purpose of breaking the bread of life. It was Jesus that said "They that hunger and thirst after righteousness shall be filled." It was also Christ that said that man "shall not live by bread alone, but every word that proceedeth out of the mouth of God." My friends, we are thankful for your presence here tonight and we hope that you have come here with open and receptive hearts that you might drink down the gospel of the Son of God, and thus become obedient to the same and be born into the family of Him who died upon Calvary. There is a great deal of talk about this doctrine. There is a great deal of discussion about the church of Christ. But I see no reason for the church of Christ and its doctrine creating such a sensation at this enlightened day, when all men and women have access to the gospel. Hardly a home in this section that hasn't a Bible in it, and my friends you may have made the sad mistake of not searching the Bible. In John 5: 39 Jesus Christ, the Lamb of God, said "Search the scriptures for in them, ye think ye have eternal life, and they are they which testify of me." The trouble with you, my people, is you haven't been searching the Bible, you haven't been searching the scriptures in earnest, when the doctrine is preached, you are not acquainted with it. You have been taught to rely upon feelings as an evidence of pardon. You have been taught to believe that you have got to go through some great excitement and emotionalism in order to become a child of God. But my friends I am of the opinion and belief that the more of the word of God you get in you, the less emotionalism, and the more of the word of God you get in you, the less excitement. You are compelled to acknowledge that this is the quietest and least emotional service that you have ever attended in your life and this is an intelligent audience, and when you accept the gospel of Jesus Christ, it knocks all the monkey notion out. And the preacher hasn't got to have a fit and run up and down the aisle like he is having a spasm—you don't have to do that—but he makes an effort to show you or prove to you he can't help it, that the Holy Ghost makes him do it. Why that creates a false impression, and I am sorry that impression has been made on the masses of the people. Then there is an objection on the part of some people about our services—that we don't have shouting. Why we don't object to shouting. I have never told anybody not to shout in a service. I have been preaching almost 29 years and in the evangelistic work 18 or 20 years, and I have never objected to a shout in my life. Why don't they shout, Brother Keeble, in your service? It's because they can't. Well, why can't they? Here is my reason. The gospel is like lead, it's heavy, when you preach it to a man, it holds him down. He can't bounce around, but when you preach a false doctrine, it is light, it's like shucks, like cotton, can't help but bounce, nothing to hold it down. But my friends, the bouncing time is over. It's time now to come down to real facts. Sit study, drink down the truth. Most of you men were raised on a farm, especially you older men, and a good many of these boys know what I am fixing to speak of as a fact.

You have been out in the barn lot, and you have seen an old sow with a number of little pigs, say for instance, 9 or 10. Nature has taught them how to notify their mother when they are hungry, and if you will watch them, they walk along beside her and they hunch her in the side, notifying her that they are ready to eat. She takes the notice well and falls down on the ground and there tells them to help themselves. Well, then each pig runs up to get his position and they do, but there is one pig in the crowd that gets a position and stays there right still and the others are changing positions and rooting one another away. That one lays right still, you needn't to worry about him, no time. You can know that he is getting results, but those pigs that are rushing across there, changing positions and bouncing across and rooting one another out, they didn't get much, because they spent their time running from position to position. And by the time the old mother thinks they ought to have had enough, she jumps up and they are not filled, because they were too busy changing; that little fellow that stayed still, he walks around all swelled up. Well, I said that, to say this. The man that goes to church and, just about the time the preacher takes his text, begins to holler Amen—before the preacher has hardly said a word—he goes away empty. And then think of the person who claims to be in possession of the Holy Ghost such that it takes two or three members to hold him, and that that emotion shows that he is filled with the Holy Ghost. Has God got a wild Holy Ghost? Why, gentlemen, it is not reasonable. I don't think any man or any woman ought to want anything that would make him hurt himself. I think if he keeps his level head, balances himself, don't need anybody to hold him. Take the modern sanctified people. They are about to dance themselves to death. Old-fashioned buck and wing dance in the service and calling it Church of God. Why friends, we can't read in the Bible nowhere since Jesus Christ died on Calvary where any of the Apostles—and the sanctified church claims to be that church that is baptized with the Holy Ghost—and you can't find where any of the Apostles who were baptized with the Holy Ghost, ever danced and rolled around. I challenge any man anywhere to show me where any Apostle ever danced or ordered dancing done, and they were baptized with the Holy Ghost. This takes it out now. The reason these preachers do it now is because they were never baptized with the Holy Ghost.

While in Tampa, Fla., in a tent meeting, a lady got up and asked permission to ask me a question; and I granted it. She wanted to know, if her religion was false, what it was that made her shout and feel so good when she went to church. I told her that a lie would make a person shout the same as the truth if he don't know it was a lie. If a man was to come here now and tell you your house was on fire, and you run home and find that he lied, could you have run any faster if he had told you the truth? What was it that made the children of Israel shout around the golden calf? (Ex. 32: 17.)

Now friends, our subject tonight is "Been to worship, but wrong." I am now standing in the presence of people, good honest people who go to worship every Sunday, no doubt you don't miss a Sunday in the year. Maybe you don't miss a prayer meeting and maybe you are just as honest to your husbands and wives as you know how to be and you go to church, pay your dues and your assessments, but you have been to worship,

BAPTISMAL SCENE AT ST. PETERSBURG, FLA.

but wrong, and I am going to refer you to a Bible
character. What I mean by that, a man who is in the
Bible that had been to worship. Went a long way to
worship and yet he was wrong. And that is the man
that we read about in the 8th Chapter of Acts, he is
called the Ethiopian eunuch, he is called the treasurer
of the Queen, and, of course, holding that kind of position, we are compelled to acknowledge that he must
have been a man highly and intellectually qualified from
an educational standpoint, to hold the position of treasurer of the Queen of the Ethiopians—he had to be undoubtedly qualified, and for that reason, he must have
been a man of some standing. Now here is a lesson.
To prove to you that he was sincere and that he was
earnest, honest and meant right, like lots of us, he went
a long way across the desert, got in his chariot and went
a long way across the desert, up to the City of Jerusalem to worship, and while he was up there at Jerusalem worshiping or on his way back, no doubt God was
making arrangements for his minister Philip, a minister of the gospel of the Son of God, to preach to him.
He has been to worship and he is returning home in his
chariot and he is busy reading—busy reading—that is
complimentary. Any man that is busy reading the
scriptures—any time—needs complimenting. And all
ought to take time to search the scriptures, because in
them we learn what God wants us to do. The eunuch
was reading Isaiah, the prophet, when Philip, the Evangelist, came along after God had sent him and got into
the chariot with him. And the Bible says that he began
at the same scripture and preached unto him, Jesus.
Now, right there I am going to make this statement,
that you can't preach Jesus, you can't preach a com-
plete Christ without getting into some water. Not

having some patted on your head—Brother Baptist, you
needn't be laughing, think you will have the joke coming on to you pretty soon. Philip began at the same
scripture and preached to him, Jesus; the passage he
was reading was this (see Isaiah 53): "He was led as
a sheep to the slaughter; and like a lamb dumb before
his shearer, so opened he not his mouth: in his humilia-
tion his judgment was taken away: and who shall de-
clare his generation? for his life is taken from the
earth." He began at that same scripture and made the
eunuch understand what the prophet was talking about,
talking about the Christ that was murdered and slain
upon the cross and suffered like a lamb on Calvary.
Philip preached that to him, and while preaching Christ
and Him crucified, the eunuch learned that there was
water in the plan, and he says "Here is water, what
hinders me from being baptized?" I am so glad the
man said "Here is water," so glad it was water you
could see, because if it wasn't, my sectarian friends
would want to oppose baptism in water, make like it
was Holy Ghost, make like it was spiritual water. It's
water that can be seen, and the Spirit you cannot see,
so I know he wasn't talking about the Spirit.

Now, gentlemen, I want you to be honest with yourselves, if you haven't done these things right, get in
your mind I am going out to the meeting and if I see
I am in error, I am going to correct it. If you haven't
made an error, don't make an error. I will do the best
I can to explain the lesson so if you have made an error,
if you are honest, you will correct it. If not, let it alone.
Then listen, Philip says unto him, "If thou believest
with all thine heart, thou mayest," and the eunuch said
to him "I believe that Jesus Christ is the Son of God."
And when the eunuch said that, what happened? When

he made this confession, the chariot stopped. What did he stop the chariot for? Got to do some baptizing. Baptism in the Bible always follows the confession; always, when that confession is made known, then comes baptism. And this eunuch, after hearing the gospel preached to him by Philip, was conscious of the fact that he had to be baptized and he wanted to know of Philip what hindered him "Here is water." And Philip said to him "If thou *believest, thou mayest," and the man opened his mouth and confessed his Saviour; and the chariot stopped, they *both* got out of the chariot and they *both* went down into the water and Philip baptized him and they both came up out of the water. I am so glad that word *"both"* is in there; because you would have made out Philip went in himself and brought out the water, but he went in with the man. And so, my friends, I want to make this statement now, that after this man was baptized, he went on his way rejoicing. If he had been a member of the sanctified church, he couldn't have left there without moaning and rolling for the Holy Ghost. I know Philip wasn't a sanctified minister, because if he had been, he would have had to hold the man trying to get the Holy Ghost, but that man goes on his way rejoicing, because, after being baptized in water, he was born again. The Bible teaches "one Lord, one faith, *one baptism;*" but Brother Sanctified teaches three baptisms, baptism in fire, baptism in water, and baptism in the Holy Ghost. Brother Sanctified is overloaded with baptism. Paul said, "one baptism." (Eph. 4: 5.) That one baptism is water baptism. In John 3: 5 Christ, the Lamb of God, says "Except a man be born of water and of the Spirit, he cannot enter into the kingdom of God." The white church at Fayetteville, Tenn., invited me there to hold a meeting for my race, as I am invited here to preach to my race, and one of the elders of the white church asked me to preach in the Court House yard on the first Monday, and I gladly accepted; because a large crowd comes to town every first Monday. My wife and one or two of the members went with me; and while we were singing, about 500 or more gathered around to see what I was going to do; and the most of them were white. After we had sung a song and had prayer, I began to preach, touching on water baptism, showing the essentiality of it and showing by the Bible that one cannot be saved without it. There was a big policeman standing in the crowd and I noticed he was paying close attention and finally he said to the men "stand back, stand back" and kept making toward me. Well, I don't like for policemen to come toward me. He kept saying "get back, get back men," and I kept preaching, but didn't take my eye off of him. Pretty soon he got in two or three feet of me and said "I want to ask you a question." When he said that, I felt pretty comfortable. "I want to ask you a question" and I said "All right, sir, Captain. I always talk nice to policemen. I said, all right, Captain, what is your question?" "I want to ask you," he said, "if you had a man to be baptized, already had his confession and you took him in an automobile to carry him to be baptized and the automobile has a wreck just before you get to the water and the young man is killed before he is baptized, what becomes of him? Is he lost or is he saved?" I said to him "according to the Bible, he is lost" and he turned away and said "I am sure you are wrong." I said "Wait a minute, Captain, will you let me ask you a question?" He came right back, "All right, what do you want to ask me?" I said, "Now Captain, did you ever know of anybody getting killed en route to baptism?" and he said "No." "Well, why pop that supposition to me? Why did you put that proposition up to me?" And he said "I just wanted to see how you looked at baptism, you appear to think it takes water baptism to save a man, I don't believe it." I said "Wait a minute, you asked me a matter of supposition, it *isn't* a fact that ever happened. Now let me ask you a question on supposition. Suppose a young man and a young lady are engaged to be married and the young man is wealthy—in that case the lady wants him quick—and they have their marriage set to come off in a few months and she gets to thinking every day that something might happen and she won't get him. She decides to ask him to marry right away and not put it off, marry and get through with it. The young man agrees, he loves her, just suits him. They go to the courthouse and they purchase a license and the young man and she lock arms and engage the County Court Clerk to marry them. He gets ready to marry them; gets ready to perform the ceremony, and the young man drops dead with heart failure. Now I have got the advantage of that policeman, he never heard of a man dropping dead on the way to baptism, but I have known a man to die with heart failure, I had him on supposition. But I asked the policeman this, "Though they were standing before the County Court Clerk about to perform a ceremony, if the County Court Clerk did not actually perform the ceremony, were they man and wife?" He said "No." "Well, what could you say in a case of that kind?" "I don't know, sir." "Yes, you could tell anybody she liked to got him." Well then, what could I say if a man should get killed before he was baptized in the name of Jesus Christ for the remission of sin? What could I say if he was killed before

he was baptized? I could tell the Judge he died before
he was baptized and he liked to have got him. Why
sure you need not take that thought that I hear in the
world today and believe that a man can be saved without being baptized. I am sorry that idea has ever crept
into the mind of anybody. I don't see how they can
conceive of that idea with the Bible as plain as it is.
Jesus said, "Except a man is born of water and the
Spirit, he cannot enter into the kingdom of God." And
some man grabs him and tries to push him in. And then
again, in baptism we marry Christ. I saw a young lady
married to Christ this morning. I heard Brother Miller
when he said the ceremony and then she was buried.
Suppose she had died before that ceremony was said.
Would she be married to Christ? That ceremony must
be said before she has any inheritance in that kingdom
He has gone to prepare. Make up your minds, the Bible
is right. You can go home and fuss all night, the Bible
is right. You can walk the streets and call Keeble a
fool, the Bible is right. You can go home and have
spasms, the Bible is right. Gentlemen, you can't get
around it, might as well come clean, the reason why the
people obeyed the Bible at Valdosta after they discov-
ered it, is because it's right. Friends, husbands and
wives accept of the Saviour and become a member of
the church bought by the blood of Jesus Christ. I know
Philip wasn't a Methodist preacher. If he had been, he
would have asked the eunuch how he wanted to be baptized. He would have said "Yes Sir, Now we have got
three kinds, what kind do you want?" Now gentlemen, that's true. If I am misrepresenting anybody, you
all raise your hands, because I don't want you to let
me get away with a misrepresentation and I know this
audience is smart enough, plenty intelligent enough to

grasp a mistake if I am misrepresenting anybody. The Methodist has three kinds—he will sprinkle you, pour you or immerse you. Now wait a minute. Here is the point I was preaching at Florence, Alabama, when old lady Beasley, a member of the A. M. E. Church and one of the oldest members of that church—had been a member 65 years—and, like the eunuch, she had been to worship lots of times and thought she was right, was on the front seat listening as close as she could. When I went over this, that the Methodists have one, two and three modes of baptism, sprinkling, pouring and immersing, old lady Beasley said "Yes, so accommodating." Why the most accommodating set of men in this town are the Methodist preachers, accommodate you to any kind of baptism you want. Ain't they nice fellows, just as nice? The only trouble, they are nice without any authority. Jesus never authorized three modes of baptism and the baptism my Bible talks about is found in Romans 6: 4. Jesus Christ, through the Apostle Paul, talking to the Roman church, said "Therefore, we are buried with him by baptism into death." Now Brother Baptist, he says Keeble is right. Brother Baptist has been buried, but he is worse off than Brother Methodist because, after he got buried and wringing wet with water, he doesn't know what it's for. Went off and got wringing wet and don't know what it was for. There is not a Baptist in this town, from the preachers on down, can tell you what he was baptized for, scripturally. He will tell you lots of things, but I say scripturally. The baptism I read about in my Bible, and it is in yours, tells me that baptism is for the remission of sin. In Acts 2: 38, Peter said "Repent, and be baptized every one of you in the name of Jesus Christ for the remission of sins, and ye shall receive the gift of the Holy Ghost."

That is written in Acts 2: 38. So my friends, we might as well come clean. Read your Bible, be honest. I hear somebody say "Brother Keeble, I don't think water has anything to do with it." Suppose you turn to Second Kings, 5th Chapter, where Naaman was told to go down and dip himself seven times in Jordan. He wanted the prophet to rub his hands over him and tell the disease to get away, but the prophet told him to dip himself in Jordan and didn't take it back. God told you to be baptized for the remission of sins and didn't take it back. He's not going to take it back. I know Philip wasn't a Baptist preacher, because if he had been a Baptist preacher, he couldn't have baptized that man by himself. A Baptist preacher can't meet a man and baptize him by himself. He's got to carry the man to the church, hear his testimony and let him be voted on. Ask any Baptist preacher if he don't have to do it. If I am wrong, come back tomorrow night and tell me. I will ask you if the eunuch was voted on, if he was not, what kind of a preacher was Philip? He was a gospel preacher. A gospel preacher can meet a man anywhere and baptize him. The very idea of trying to vote on a man and sometimes sending him back for God to work him over! I am ashamed before God the way my race has been butchered; the way the gospel is butchered.

I must commend you for coming to listen to the messages. It shows you must appreciate these messages and that you get the benefit of them. I hope you will.

Now friends, in conclusion, I want to say are there any of you that want to come to Jesus as this eunuch did? Are there any of you almost persuaded? I thank God that the white disciples invited me, furnished the tent, furnished the chairs and had me to come and preach to you the pure word of God. We thank God for the wonderful gospel that is being preached to my race as never before and the church of Christ is doing that. We are glad to reach out, my friends, with that gospel that the Apostle Paul preachéd and bring you to Jesus Christ. I hope there is somebody waiting for that invitation song to be sung; that somebody is sitting willing and waiting to walk out and become a member of that church bought by the blood of the Lamb on these conditions:

1. Jesus said, in Mark 12: 29, "The first of all commandments is, Hear, O Israel: The Lord our God is one Lord."

2. In Hebrews 11: 6, Apostle Paul said, "But without faith it is impossible to please him; for he that cometh to God must believe that he is, and that he is a rewarder of them that diligently seek him."

3. I move on up to repentance. Jesus Christ in Luke 13: 3 said "Except ye repent, ye shall also likewise perish." Somebody wants to know what is repentance. Repentance is, if you have been beating your wife, quit. If you have been stealing, quit. If you have been bothering John's wife, let her alone. If you have been bothering Sal's husband, let him alone. What you do when you do that; that is repentance. There are plenty of you here tonight under this tent claiming to have religion, taking one another's wives and husbands; and go to church and shout like a limber jack. Many women in this town that claim to be Christians, are meeting some of you men that claim to have religion and taking the bread out of the little children's mouths. The reason you do it, you have never repented. Repentance means quit your meanness.

In Isaiah 55: 7, "Let the wicked forsake his way, and the unrighteous men his thoughts, and let him return unto the Lord, and he will have mercy upon him, and to our God, for he will abundantly pardon." In Ezekiel, 18th Chapter, it is said "If the wicked will turn from all his sins that he hath committed, and keep all my statutes, and do that which is lawful and right, he shall surely live, he shall not die." When men repent, they quit.

4. Next is confession. The eunuch said, "I believe that Jesus is the Christ, the Son of God."

5. (See Acts 2: 38.) Baptism is for the remission of sins, and ye shall receive the gift of the Holy Ghost. And in Acts 22: 16, "Arise, and be baptized, and wash away thy sins." Are there any of you tonight willing to come, almost persuaded? I ask you in the name of Israel's God; in the name of Him who hung upon the cross of Calvary between the twilight of two worlds; in the name of Him who said I am the Alpha and the Omega; in the name of Him that said I am He that was dead and am alive again. Will you come?

Will you come to Him, dear friends, when this invitation is extended?

Five Steps TO THE CHURCH

Seven Steps TO HEAVEN

PURE RELIGION

SANCTIFIED LIFE

C.
B.
G.
P.
T.
K.
V.

CHURCH OF CHRIST

B.
C.
R.
B.
H.

Jesus Says, "Come Unto Me"

CHAPTER IV.

———

FIVE STEPS TO THE CHURCH AND SEVEN STEPS TO HEAVEN.

———

We thank God for this great and splendid audience that have assembled here this evening. We trust for the purpose of getting a better understanding, a more clearer conception of the gospel of Jesus Christ. If there ever was a time that people should begin to investigate the blessed truth of the gospel of Christ and understand thoroughly just those things that are required of them to do in order to inherit eternal life, it is now. Eternity is too long and death is too certain and sure for us to waste away our time with creeds and disciplines of man. We are conscious of the fact that we are to be judged in the last day, and that the book of God, the book divine, will be opened and all nations, kindred and tongues judged therefrom. It has been circulated and is now being circulated among the people of Valdosta that the reason there are so many accepting of the gospel in this meeting is because there is a trick in it. The devil is busy. Some reports have gone out that if you don't want to join the church of Christ, and of course you can't join the church of Christ, you can join these other churches and if you don't pay your dues, they will un-join you. You can weep and cry, but out you go. And any institution that man can turn you out of won't do to risk for salvation. You can't join the church of Christ; God adds to the church daily such as should be saved, Acts 2: 47. They say if you go to the tent and get any ways close to Keeble, he will throw out some stuff and you can't help but go up there. Now that, of itself, that of itself is enough to show you that we are living in the worst suspicious age that has ever existed. You are full of hoodooism, witchcraft and all kinds of craftiness. And folks, you are full of it; you imagine I come here with it. I have brought to you the gospel of the Son of God. I have told you where to go and read these truths. I never come here acting like I thought I was some great I Am. I came humbly and meekly offering you the gospel, endeavoring to help you develop into the kind of character that God wants you to be. And if you can go home and read the things that I am teaching in your Bibles, if its hoodooism, it was God who hoodooed you.

I remember being in a meeting at Summit, Ga., about six years ago. There was an old lady, whose name was Sister Clarke. I forget her first name. She was a member of the Methodist Church for 55 years. I went into that section conducting a meeting similar to this, and she, as well as I can remember, sit on the front seat each night and she had two little grandchildren, seemingly about 11 or 12 years of age, one sit on one side of her and the other on the other side, and they had a tablet and pencil and as I would quote the Scriptures, the little things would scratch down something on the tablets that they had. I wondered what they were doing, being so small. I wondered about it. And after the third or fourth night of the meeting, Sister Clarke walked out and gave me her hand and demanded baptism for the remission of her sins. After I baptized her, I then approached her and asked her what were those children doing that was sitting beside her. She said she had them jotting down the passages of Scripture because she couldn't read and she wasn't acquainted with me, but her little children she had utmost confidence in, and she said several nights those little children were up until about two o'clock in the morning trying to find those passages for grandma. And the poor little things not being acquainted with the Bible, couldn't find the passages as well as one that was acquainted with it and it taken them some time, but they never went to sleep until they read every passage to grandma. She said the reason she had them reading to her and finding it was that she didn't know me and she didn't know whether I was lying or not. I said "Well, I thank you." I would suggest that you all do this like those children, like Grandma Clarke did. She was criticized. Her pastor criticized her, went to her house and told her he thought she had some sense, and she said "I thought I did too, but I found out you had misled me." That is the trouble with this town, your pastors, and your moderators, and your superintendents or presiding elders, and your deacons and stewards ought to read the Bible so they wouldn't lead the masses astray. There is your trouble. I am not responsible for what they have done to you. If the things that you have did can't be found in the Bible, don't jump on me, go get the fellow that misled you and ask him "What did you do that for?" Don't go jumping on me. I have never done nothing to you. I come here trying to straighten you. You are crooked, don't want to be straightened. Puts me in mind of a mule a man had once. The traces were twisted and a knot got in the traces, it was irritating the mule, and the man that had sent for the mule wanted to help the mule and he stepped up to take the knot out of the traces and the mule kicked him. You can't help a mule. Now, I don't mean I can't help you, but it's awful hard. I am here and I wouldn't like to compare you with that mule, but I am trying hard to take the knot out of your traces, religiously. You have a knot in your traces and I am trying to unhitch you and you won't let me. Some o' you out there now are too stubborn to change. You are like the old lady in Louisville, Ky., who believed the doctrine that I was preaching, but said she didn't want to change from her church. She told me she never believed in jumping from limb to limb. And I told her she was right, providing the limb she was sitting on was a sound one; but if it was rotten it would be unwise to remain perched on a rotten limb. When the limb is so rotten it is cracking, it is time to change. Folks here in this audience trying to sit on the dead and rotten limbs of man-made creeds and disciplines and manuals, and they're cracking right now under you. You better change. Wise bird don't roost on a rotten limb.

Now, the subject tonight is "Five Steps to the Church and Seven Steps to Heaven." That is the subject for tonight. I hope as I treat this subject as best I know how and with as much love as I am able to command and with as much humbleness and meekness as I am able to exhibit, I shall deliver this lesson regardless of your fitness, or regardless of your thoughts or ideas— I shall deliver this lesson like the Bible teaches it, trusting that somebody in this audience will be intelligent enough to accept of the truth, lay down mother's religion, lay down father's religion, lay down everything that exalts itself against God, and thus surrender and become obedient to the things God would have you to do and thus become His child.

I have here on this diagram two ladders, one of these ladders reaches down from the church into the world and that ladder we would like to call it, Ladder No. 1.

We have in the church a ladder that Christians climb en
route to heaven and if you stay on that Ladder No. **2,**
after getting in the church, you can't miss heaven. A
guarantee goes with it. Here is the trouble with my
modern sanctified friends. Poor things are trying to
climb Ladder No. 2 and have never climbed Ladder No.
1, don't know nothing about it. Our good old Methodist and Baptist friends haven't even started. According to scriptures they're not trying to climb neither one
of these ladders. Brother Sanctified's crowd is trying
to climb No. 2 but don't know nothing about No. 1.
Now we shall take our time and deal with this question
carefully, because you certainly need to know what to
do and how to climb these ladders. Now every man
and every woman must climb Ladder No. 1 before they
can become members of the church of Christ. In Matthew 16: 18, when Jesus came into the coasts of Cæsarea
Philippi and asked the question, "Whom do men say
that I, the Son of man, am?" and Simon Peter answered
and said "Thou art the Christ, the Son of the living
God." In the 17th and 18th verses "flesh and blood
hath not revealed it unto thee, but my Father which is
in heaven, upon this rock I will build my church." That
church is a future church. "I will" is a future thing. I
met a Baptist preacher not long ago trying to tell me
that John the Baptist established a church, but I told
him to read Matthew 16: 18 and he would find that
John the Baptist's head had been cut off and he was
dead and yet the church was a future institution. John
was dead when Christ said "I will;" bled and died before the church of Christ came into existence. John
never was in it. I am today blessed with the privilege
of being in an institution that John the Baptist never
was permitted to get in. A member of the church of

Christ that was built after the beheading of John the Baptist. I shall talk about John the Baptist a little more as the meeting progresses. You tell all those Baptist preachers I said so. Well, you need not tell them. They are all around out there somewhere. You could go out there just behind those cars and run over ten or fifteen of them. Now friends, I don't only mean Baptist preachers, you will find all the preachers in town; Christian Church preacher is back out there; Methodist preacher is out there somewhere. I am glad of the fact that I can come into your town and preach a naked gospel that the preachers of the town can hear. Christ hath already said "That the heavens that now be and the earth will pass away but His word stands forever," and I hear John talking on the Isle of Patmos, says that some day the stars that shine in the sky, some day the mountains that reach across the earth will move gently out of their places, some day the rocks that now be will melt with fervent heat, but the word of God stands forever. The word of God is all that is not going to be moved. So I am rooted; I am grounded on that everlasting word and mean to stay there until my Master makes his second return back to the earth again. Then I hope to go with Him back to that eternal city that He has gone to prepare.

Now friends, the first round in this ladder, Round No. 1. Jesus says the first commandment is to hear, (Mark 12: 29.) The second round in the ladder is belief, 11th Chapter Hebrews and 6th verse. There is a great deal of argument and contention about how we get faith, but there ought not to be. There is not a plainer passage in this Bible than the passage that tells us how we get faith. You have been taught that you had to pray for faith. Well, friends, the Apostle Paul in Romans

10: 17, says faith comes by hearing. You don't have to pray for it. It don't come that way, faith comes by hearing, and hearing by the word of God. You don't have to pray for it. You just hear that Christ died, hear He was buried, and you ought to hear He was raised from the dead, and when you have heard that you have heard the gospel. In the 15th Chapter of First Corinthians, beginning with the first two or three verses, you will be informed that the gospel is the death, and the burial, and the "resurrection" of Jesus Christ. When a man hears that Christ died, that he was buried and that he was raised from the dead, he has heard the gospel and when that same character believes that, he has believed what he heard. What did he hear? Gospel, well that is what he believes and it comes by hearing. Don't you catch it?

Now friends, the third step, the third round in the ladder is repentance. Jesus Christ, the Lamb of God, had the Apostle Peter, through the guidance of the Holy Ghost, to write upon the pages of the book of inspiration "Repent, and be baptized every one of you in the name of Jesus Christ for the remission of sins." (Acts 2: 38.) You must repent, and what is repentance? Repentance is a reformation of life. A man who has decided to quit his devilment. Did you not know that if Uncle Sam, our great United States Government, were spending one-third of the money that they are spending to enforce prohibition, to spend that to bring men to Christ and to have the gospel preached, why prohibition would be a great thing. And the gospel of Jesus Christ is the only thing that will stop men from sinning. It has already been proven that jail houses won't stop it; penitentiaries have got to be enlarged, our United States Government are enlarging all Federal prisons, and yet they are crowded. The last reports are they are flooded and more room must be made. The State penitentiaries are crowded and your jail houses are flooded and the only thing to stop men from sinning is the gospel of Christ. The electric chair won't stop them, hanging won't stop them, and the only thing that will stop them, gentlemen, is what the Apostle Paul had in mind when he said "I am not ashamed of the gospel of Christ, for it is the power of God unto salvation to every one that believeth." (Romans 1: 16.) It is powerful enough to stop a man from bootlegging, it is powerful enough to stop a man from beating his wife, it is powerful enough to make him stay away from his neighbor's wife, and it is powerful enough to make a woman let her neighbor's husband alone. When you don't, you haven't repented. I don't see my friends how you can make like you have religion and live like you are living. You are going to have to give an account for the way you are living. You are going to have to give an account for the way you treat your neighbor. He says "Love your neighbor as yourself." No man that loves his neighbor as himself will wreck another man's home. And no woman that loves her husband and loves her home and loves herself will murder another woman and cause her to go to the grave before her time.

And then after hearing, and believing and repentance, then confession, Round No. 4. One lady said to me when I was preaching in Houston, Texas, a few months ago, I began to treat the subject of repentance like this and she arose up and said "My God man, why haven't you been here before now." Why you people need this, the preachers today are are not preaching on these vital principles. Why they have got to have some money and the best paying members are the ones doing all this, singing in the choir, sitting in the Amen corner. Now once more, just a minute, gentlemen, listen: The next round in the ladder is confession. You ought to have been taught to confess Christ, but you were not, you were taught to profess religion and you did that and I have never known anybody to profess religion that didn't tell too much. Generally say they seen a little man, said a man beckoned "Come here." Some of you seen a star shoot, some seen an angel, you have seen too much. Jesus Christ, the Lamb of God, said to the Apostle Paul, 11th chapter of Hebrews, "that faith is the substance of things hoped for, the evidence of things not seen." He told you "not seen." There is your trouble, you have seen too much. When you got through you really hadn't seen nothing. If you wasn't ashamed you would stand up and say "Brother Keeble, you are right, I never seen nothing." Well what did you tell it for? "I told it because I had to tell it to get in the church, and the bigger tale I could tell, the more I would impress them that I had it." If you tell only a little bit of something, they will send you back for God to work over.

Then, after confessing Christ, you are taught to be baptized in water. Now my friends, my good religious and sanctified friends say that it is the Holy Ghost that sanctifies you, but I read in the Bible what it is that sanctifies us. In the 5th chapter of the Book of Ephesians, verses 25, 26, Apostle Paul says "Husbands, love your wives!" That passage is too good to run over and as I quote that passage, you men will know whose wife to love. "Husbands, love *your* wives," and the average man will love his wife and she will love him and be true to him and honest, no doubt, and maybe raise a

number of children for him, then he gets tired of her;
the next thing, he leaves the children and her to go
running around looking for somebody that don't care
nothing about him. "Husbands, love your wives, even
as Christ also loved the church, and gave himself for it"
—here it comes—"that he might *sanctify* and *cleanse* it."
Does two things—"*sanctifies*" it and "cleanses" it with
the "washing of water by the word." That is when I got
sanctified nearly 39 years ago, it will be in October. I
was baptized and washed in water and I knew that I
was sanctified and cleansed with the "washing of water
by the word."

And then listen, hearing, believing, repentance, confession and baptism put us into Christ. When you get
in Christ, in Galatians 3: 27, the Apostle Paul says,
"For as many of you as have been baptized into Christ
have put on Christ. *Baptized into Christ,* that is the
way we get into Christ by and through the process of
baptism. I want to say, ladies, gentlemen, friends,
brethren and sisters, there is not a passage in the Bible
treating on any subject that puts a man into Christ except baptism. Not a man in this town can introduce
any other passage, any other thing that puts a man into
Christ aside from baptism. That is the reason the church
of Christ contends that without baptism you can't be
saved; because you can't be saved outside of Christ, and
you can't get into Him without baptism. Well then,
after getting into the church, you have got to climb
Ladder No. 2, get up that ladder by climbing it round
by round. Apostle Peter, in the second Epistle of Peter,
1st chapter, says this, that after you have been baptized
to "add to your faith, virtue," Round No. 1, Ladder
No. 2, and after you add virtue, then in Round No. 2,
add "knowledge," and after you have added "knowl-

edge," then add "temperance," and after you have
added "temperance," then add "patience," and after
you have added "patience," add "godliness," and after
you have added "godliness," add "brotherly kindness,"
and after you have added "brotherly kindness," add
"charity," and the Apostle says if a man does those
things, he shall never fall." If this is not sanctification,
climbing that ladder, what is sanctification? What is
climbing that ladder for? If somebody falls off that ladder, he don't tell you to get back and climb Ladder No.
1; you must repent and get back on the ladder and
continue until death. You didn't know that? Brother
Sanctified don't understand this ladder. He makes like
he can't fall off. Yes you can, and God made pro-
vision so His child can come back and get back on it
and try it again. If you fall off of No. 2, repent and
get back on, it's just as plain as can be.

Now in conclusion, I wish to say that I hope there is
some precious soul in this audience that is not ashamed
to come out of denominationalism and sectarian teaching and take a decided stand and say, "I am going to
my Saviour, I give myself to Thee, it's all that I can
do. I know I am going to be criticized for this act.
I know the world is going to point the finger of
scorn, but they pointed it at my Saviour and I am satisfied they will point it at me." Somebody says, "I am
going the way my mother went." Thank God, Jesus
said "if a man loves father and mother more than me
he is not worthy of me." My friends you are going to
have to give up father and mother, give up former
teaching and take the word of God for your guide.
And again, some day when you fall asleep and are con-
signed to the narrow limits of the earth, your parents,
your wives, your children can follow you to the ceme-

tery and there look down the sepulcher as the clods are thrown in upon your casket, and when the clods have been put down upon it, wives, children, father and mother go home and in a few years forget you ever lived. But thank God, if you serve Jesus Christ, He will never forsake you. He will never forsake you. David the Psalmist said, "Though I walk through the valley of the shadow of death, I will fear no evil: for thou art with me; thy rod and thy staff they comfort me." Oh how sweet it is to give up the world for the Man that did so much for us, hung on the cross, shed his own precious blood, left heaven and the habitation of the angels and came down and made himself poor and said: "Foxes have holes and the birds of the air have got a nest; but the Son of man have got nowhere to lay his head." Suffered and become poor that I might live. Going down in the grave, wrestling with the devil, He came out victorious and declared that I have got all power in the heavens and the earth. If you claim your sins are pardoned before baptism, you deny the teachings of the Holy Spirit; you deny the teachings of God Almighty, deny the teachings of Jesus Christ. He promised you pardon in baptism. (Mark 16: 15, 16; Acts 2: 38; Acts 22: 16; 1 Peter 3: 21; John 3: 5; Ephesians 5: 25-27.)

This afternoon, before we came to worship, three precious people came and demanded baptism, with a bundle of clothes under their arms, and made the confession. One woman said, "I couldn't rest all night." When the doctrine of the Son of God gets in your head, there is no rest until you obey. May God Almighty help you to see it as these three precious souls have that came with their bundles under their arms. But how my heart leaped for joy when I seen Brother Miller bury them underneath the waves, having their sins blotted out and the time of refreshing will come from the presence of the Lord. My heart leaped for joy. And will not you confess your Saviour and be baptized because you have never been baptized for the remission of your sins? The invitation is extended while we stand.

NOTHING TOO HARD FOR THE LORD.

1. N—Healed.

2. Walls of J. thrown down.

3. World destroyed with water.

4. Crossing the Red Sea.

(This above was for the people before Christ came.)

HAVE YOU BEEN BAPTIZED FOR REMISSION
OF SINS?

(This is for us today.)

CHAPTER V.

___

"NOTHING TOO HARD FOR THE LORD."

___

We thank you, my friends, for your splendid gath-
ing here tonight, and we want to thank you again for
the interest that you are manifesting in these meetings. And above all, we thank God for his guidance and
for his protection while we attempt to break unto you
the bread of life, God's eternal word. And we hope tonight when the privilege is granted, when you are
given the opportunity to respond to the invitation of
the Lord Jesus Christ, that there will be many of you
who will have a sufficient amount of courage and boldness to come forward and confess your Lord and
Saviour, Jesus Christ. It is being said by many of you
that if this doctrine is right, what have become of all
the old-timey people that have died and gone before
this came? Now, that is a question that nobody in the
world can decide, what became of all the old-time people that died before this gospel was preached in Valdosta? I can't tell, you can't tell, and it will take God
to tell at the judgment; but I am forced to believe that
if the old-time people that you have reference to had all
heard this gospel preached as I am endeavoring to do,
as honest as they were, they would have accepted it
long ago. They wouldn't be as stubborn as you are, I
don't believe they would. Then there is another feature
about it, you are not as interested in the old-time people
as you propose to be, because many of you are the cause
of the old-timey people being dead. You young people
today are rushing your old parents into the grave rap-

idly because of disobedience. Many of you little girls
sitting here with knee dresses on (of course, the old
women are wearing them too), but many of you young
ladies think you can walk out from home without asking anybody any privilege at all, stay out at any hour of
the night, make mother roll and rock on the bed; and
she is soon carried to the cemetery. And you jump up
and down and holler, "What became of mamma?" You
have killed her, that's what. Now friends, you need not
worry about the old-timey people. If they died prepared, you have nothing to do with it. If they died un-
prepared, you and I have nothing to do with it. You
are living in an age in which you are responsible indi-
vidually for yourselves. You are trying to imitate your
parents in some respects; but in many respects, you are
not. Away back yonder they wore dresses that dragged
the ground, and they had on so much they could hardly
walk, and now you hardly wear over a pound or a pound
and a half. So you needn't to worry about your parents, look after yourself. If she was back here now
trying to exist, you would call her an old fogy, and you
are making fun of the parents you got now. Now you
all be quiet; don't answer so much, and I can talk better.
I want you folks to drink this message. We came here
to get the truth to the hearts of the people and I am
sincere and I am in sympathy with my fellow man that
has been misled. And so friends, I want to tell you
about my precious old mother; and you need to do like
I did. Instead of following my mother into things that
she couldn't read in the Bible, and neither could I, I
went and learned the Bible as best I could and obeyed
the gospel and then went back and tried to get my
mother. Then finally after obeying the gospel, I began
to preach and I would write letters back to her, calling

her attention to her mistakes, religiously, and when I
would come home and go over to see my mother, I
would bring up a religious conversation in order to get
to tell her about her mistake. And sometimes she would
tell me to "shut up, you are getting too mannish." And
me with several children, getting "mannish." But any-
how, sometimes she would draw back her hand to strike
me, to hit me in the mouth, and I would have to let up
on that. Then I would come back later on and find her
in a good humor and make another strike at her. I kept
my mother on my mind. I didn't want her to die in the
condition that she was in. So once she came over to
my home and she told my wife—she called me "Marsh,"
my name is Marshall, and she called me Marsh, cut it
off short, and she told my wife "You tell Marsh to hurry
home, I want to hear him preach once more." Well,
I wondered about that. I was in a meeting something
similar to this and I hurried home, closed the meeting
as quick as I could and went home and preached on
Sunday about five years ago, and after I preached that
Sunday morning, my mother came walking down the
aisle when the invitation was extended, and I couldn't
wait for her to come to me, I ran and grasped her in
my arms. There we wept a few minutes. When we
came to ourselves, became composed, she sat down.
After she made the confession, I asked when she wanted
to be baptized. She said "right now." I asked her if
she wanted me to do it. She said "nobody else." And
with these hands I buried my mother in the watery
grave of baptism for the remission of sins. And I don't
think, of the almost six thousand I have baptized in the
last few years, that I ever did a greater work than I
did when I took hold of my mother and buried her in
baptism for the remission of her sins. I said that to

say this, instead of you children dropping into super-
stition and false doctrine with your parents, learn the
gospel and go back and get them who are misled,
slaughtered by gospel butchers.

This meeting is one of the most interesting meetings
I have ever held. We are only four nights old in the
meeting and there have been 45 confessions in only
four nights, tonight makes five. No telling how many
are waiting now to make the confession. I hope that
there are lots of you. There have been seven more
confessions since we left here last night. People keep
coming with bundles under their arms; two ladies
walked up to me today, I was busy writing, they said
"Brother Keeble, you know what we come for," didn't
ask to be baptized; had the bundle and said "you
know," and I am satisfied I knew and I said "In
a minute we will be ready;" and before they could be
baptized, we had to run the water in the pool, as we
had emptied it and had to fill it with fresh water. While
we were doing that, somebody must have told a lady
up the street somewhere for she came running with a
bundle. So it's all right. The more you fuss about it,
the more you grumble, the faster it grows. In fact, the
truth won't do much until somebody bothers it. I am
here tonight to preach to you, and listen what the subject is, diagrammed on the chart, "Is There Anything
too Hard for the Lord?" That is the subject tonight.
While we discuss this subject, I hope you will watch
closely as we go from one point to another and see if
there is anything too hard for the Lord.

The first case that we call your attention to is away
back in the old Bible. There was a man by the name
of Naaman, who was Captain of the Syrian Army, who
was afflicted with the leprosy, with a disease that was

contagious; with a disease that was catching, and naturally this man wanted to get rid of that disease. He
learned, through a little Hebrew maid captured by the
Syrian Army, of a man by the name of Elisha, a prophet
of the Lord God Almighty, that could cure him or give
him a remedy. So Naaman gets ready, gets in his
chariot and he goes off down to Elisha's home, and
when he gets there, Elisha sends his messenger out to
tell Naaman to dip seven times in water in the River
Jordan. And Naaman being somewhat of the disposi-
tion of the average man today, didn't want to dip in
Jordan. The Bible says he got wroth, got mad like
you people are. When I came into this town last year,
instead of accepting God's remedy, you got mad, some
of you; and today somebody is mad at Valdosta about
the remedy that God gave for sins. But Naaman said
he wanted the prophet to come out and rub his hands
over him and to bid the disease to depart, rub it off
like you all want pardon from sins. Yes, you want to
go to the mourners' bench or to some stump down in
the valley, just the place where you want to go. God
has told you where sins would be pardoned, and I am
going to tell you later on right where it happens, whether
you like it or not. And now then, Naaman sit out in
the chariot mad; and after he decided to dip in water,
he didn't like the place that God sent him and he wanted
to go to the Rivers of Damascus, where the water was
pretty and clear, and rejects the Jordan, doubtless on
the ground that it was muddy. Now you today want
to go to some other place to get cured of sins, you
reject God's remedy, God's plan, to get a prescription
for sin. And why do you do it? It's because you reject God's word and fight against the law of God.

Jesus Christ says in the 7th chapter of Matthew, 21st

verse, "Not every one that saith unto me, Lord, Lord, shall enter the kingdom of heaven; but he that doeth the will of my Father which is in heaven." You have got to obey the law of God, gentlemen, and God wouldn't change his plan for Naaman, although he was Captain of the Syrian Army, and the God that I serve and you serve today will not change his plan for Mr. Hoover, one of the greatest statesmen in the world today. God's plan must stand; God's remedy for sins will not be changed for no man. So then friends, Naaman finally decided that he would go to Jordan and dip; and he went to Jordan, dipped down once, dipped down twice, dipped down three times, dipped the fourth time, the fifth, the sixth. Is the leprosy gone? No, Sir. Why? Because God said seven, and six has not removed it; it will take seven dips to move it, and when he went down in the water of Jordan the last time, which was seven times, and come up, the leprosy was gone. I would like to ask this intelligent audience, who was it that cured Naaman? It was God you say and you are correct. Who did he heal him through? Who did he use in conveying the prescription or the remedy to him? He used his servant, Elisha. Then what have we got? We have got the One that healed him; we have got the man He used to tell him where the healing was to take place; got those two things. The next question is, what did He heal him with? What did he heal him with? The same Bible that says God healed him, and the same Bible that says Elisha gave him the message, that same Bible tells us what God healed him with—that water in the Jordan. Water did it. God used water and you haven't got a thing to do with it. You here asking me what is in the water? None of your business, you get in there yourself and then you will be in Christ. And now then; Why, Naaman could have asked this question: What has the Jordan got, that you want me to dip in, to cure the leprosy? He could have asked that. What is in the water that you want me to be baptized for the remission of sins? That is what you ask, my friends. You have no right or authority, you poor weak, frail, human beings, to call God in question. So when Naaman came up the seventh time, the leprosy was all gone. When he went down in the water the last time and come up, it was gone and his skin back like that of a little child. You say, where did the leprosy get away? In Jordan. The same place where his leprosy got away, the same place your sins get away. The same One done that job can do your job, and He will do your job if you comply with His law. That's a wonderful job God did there with the River Jordan, nobody in town disputes that, none of the preachers will tell you that God didn't heal Naaman in Jordan. No Sir, they won't. I have confidence in these distinguished pastors—the distinguished gentlemen—and I believe that they will tell you that Naaman was cleansed in the Jordan. I don't think there is a preacher in town that will deny that. I have great confidence in them.

Another wonderful job that God did was the throwing down of the walls of Jericho, way back yonder in the days of the Israelites during the prophetic age, Joshua was ordered by God to march around the walls of Jericho once a day for six days, then on the seventh day march around the walls of Jericho seven times, blow a ram's horn and give a shout and down would go the wall. Had it been you, you would have said this; you would have told Joshua to pray while marching. God never said nothing about praying as he

marched around. The fact is, you've always done too
much. God tells you to do one thing and you do another. And now then, when they marched around the
walls on the seventh day, down came the walls, and it
was God that threw them down, but it was on the conditions that they do what He told them to do, and thus
they did.

We come to another wonderful work, another wonderful job. Away back during the antediluvian period,
during the days before the flood when God decided he
would destroy man from the face of the earth because
of man's transgression. God repented that He had
made man, and if you please, I would like to inform you
that out of everything that God has ever made, He has
never regretted that He made nothing but man, and I
believe he is about the worst thing He made. Now
friends, God decided to send the flood upon the earth
to wash men off the earth. Your attention is called to
this work. God found a man by the name of Noah;
and he told Noah to build an ark and to build it out
of gopher wood, certain dimensions wide, certain dimensions long and certain dimensions high, and Noah was
a long time erecting or building that ark, and I want to
ask you all, who are so worried about the old-time people,
how many people got in the ark? You are so excited!
Uh! That will answer your question, won't it? What
became of the old-time people that didn't go in the ark?
Uh! What became of them? You know as well as
you are sitting out there what became of all the old-time
people that didn't go in the ark, and if I mistake not,
Jesus says "As it was in the days of Noah, so shall it be
in the days of the coming of the Son of man." So you
needn't get excited about your old-time people. Out of
the whole great big world, poor old Noah, faithful, old,

righteous preacher, he couldn't get but seven folks to
believe what he preached, the rest laughed and made
fun of him, and some, no doubt, got mad like you are
doing here in Valdosta. Preachers caucus and members caucus. I pass by some on the street and say
"Howdy do." One poke his mouth out because I told
him howdy. I laugh, I smile, because I know he don't
know any better, wouldn't do it if he was all right.
Listen friends, when Noah went into the ark, God
wouldn't let Noah shut the door. God shut the door
Himself. Why wouldn't he let him shut it? If God
had permitted Noah to shut it, he, no doubt, would have
cracked it and said "Hop in papa, hop in grandma."
And he would have had all of his people in there and
that would have ruined that ark. God shut the door
Himself. You take the people in these churches—I hate
to hear any preacher get up before an audience and
talk about he is going to open the doors of the
church. I wonder what kind of church he is going to
open the doors of. Then I wonder again and I say
this: "Yes, he can open it." How can he open it?
It's his own and he can do what he wants to with it.
But the church of Christ door can't be opened because
it was opened nearly two thousand years ago, never
been shut since. Wide open, and when it is shut again,
it will take Jesus to come back again and shut it. I
know you have been going in the door that man opened.
Now then, this ark floated upon the bosom of the water
and Peter, looking down the stream of time, pointing
back to the ark, says, in the 3rd chapter of the 1st
Epistle of Peter, 20th verse: "When once the long
suffering of God waited in the days of Noah, while the
ark was a preparing, wherein few, that is, eight souls
were saved by water. The like figure whereunto even

baptism doth also now save us." Apostle Peter said that, and you people can't deny the statement, because with this statement it says "Not the putting away of the filth of the flesh, but the answer of a good conscience toward God." I want to say that no man's conscience is good until his sins are pardoned. And is it not baptism where your sins are pardoned? Therefore, prepare to be baptized in the name of Jesus Christ for the remission of sins, for when a man comes out of the water, sins forgiven, his conscience is good. It is necessary to have a good conscience, and his conscience wouldn't be clear—good—if his sins were not forgiven.

I believe I will state this: Brother Methodist, I don't mean any harm, it's just a little thought dropped for your especial benefit. John the Baptist said "I indeed baptize you with water unto repentance: but he that cometh after me is mightier than I, whose shoes I am not worthy to bear: he shall baptize you with the Holy Ghost, and with fire." Brother Methodist, what about the word "with?" It means to apply. Let me look at that word "with!" In the case where God destroyed the whole world with the flood, it was done "with" water. That was a splendid job, and you know they were covered up: that they were drowned "with" water. You see that just as plain as can be and that job was done *with* water. At Tampa, Florida, a few years ago, preaching the doctrine, I told the people "I am going to preach tonight, regardless of what you say; regardless of whether you like it or not. I am going to preach the gospel of the Son of God," when an old lady, Sister Bradley, rose up in the middle of the audience and said "Brother Keeble, preach the word, and before you stop preaching the word, eat it up." I said "Yes, before I will quit, I will eat it up."

Now then, another wonderful job that God did, and that was delivering the children of Israel from Egyptian bondage. He led them in the daytime by a pillar of cloud and in the night time by a pillar of fire; and today, instead of us being led by a pillar of fire or by a pillar of cloud, we are led by God's unerring counsel. The word of God, Apostle Paul says, is quick and powerful, sharper than a two-edged sword, as the old colored man said "it cuts coming and a-gwine." My friends, I want to say that God led the children of Israel out of bondage and Moses came to the Red Sea with over a half million people, grown men, besides women and children. I am going to ask you, since you are so disturbed over the old-time people, how many of that six hundred thousand who left Egypt with Moses entered the promised land? How many out of that 600,000 able-bodied men, besides women and children, entered the promised land? Only two, Joshua and Caleb. What became of the old timers? You are so disturbed over the old timers. And now then, my Bible teaches me that these old timers left Egypt and got hardheaded and disobedient and got killed in the wilderness. Who killed them and who will kill you and send your soul to eternal torment if you don't obey Him, God? Just a minute and I am through. These four things [pointing] that God did. Splendid things, wonderful works. "There is nothing too hard for the Lord." Do you believe that God led the children of Israel across the Red Sea? Do you believe that Moses stood on the bank and stretched his rod out over the sea and the sea parted clear across and congealed on both sides, so that the children of Israel marched through dry shod? Then the enemy came and found the opening in the Red Sea, and Pharaoh's host plunged in after them and would have overtaken them, but God caused the chariot wheels to roll heavy and he told Moses to stretch his rod over the sea and the water came together and destroyed the enemy of God's people. Now you believe that God destroyed the world with a flood of water. You also believe that God threw down the walls of Jericho after the children of Israel marched around them according to his instructions; and you also believe that God healed Naaman when he dipped in Jordan seven times. Well now then, if you can believe all that, isn't it remarkably strange you can't believe this on the bottom of this chart? [Points.] This on the bottom concerns us. I mention this case as an example to show you how God can do anything that He wants to do. He is able to do it, nothing too hard for the Lord. God gives pardon in baptism for remission of sins. But you don't believe He can do it. Do you? You are trying to make like He can't do it, but He can do it. If he could heal Naaman by dipping in Jordan seven times, He can do that. Baptism is yours and dipping was Naaman's. And if He could throw the walls of Jericho down by the children of Israel marching around it as He ordered, He can do that. [Points.] And if He could drown or destroy the whole world with a flood, excepting eight souls, He can do that [points] for you, and if he could lead his children across the Red Sea and destroy the enemy in the waters of the Red Sea, he can do this [points] for you. God can do it. He is able to do it if you will comply with His law.

Now, I believe I will say this—I don't think anybody in town will bother me—I don't think you will do it— I liked to have said, I dare you to bother me. I believe I will say it. And now then, I dare any preacher to bother this statement I am fixing to make. Of course you needn't tell these preachers that I said it because they are all out there now, and just time we dismiss, they break off home before you can catch them and will be home sitting on the porch, looking like they have been nowhere. I am fixing to say this: God Almighty took water and baptized this whole earth during the antediluvian period and rained water down on earth forty days and nights and when God got through raining water down upon the earth, it stayed on the earth several months; and when the water was cleared away, Noah stepped out of the ark on a clean earth—God had cleansed it. If God can take water and cleanse the whole world, He can take water and wash our sins away. And God can do that. "There's nothing too hard for the Lord," if we obey.

Listen friends, away back yonder during the days of the Apostles, there was a man by the name of Saul. He was a man that made havoc of the church. He was a man that done much evil to God's children, but when God got ready to stop him, he made one of the greatest servants out of him that ever made footprints on the earth. Saul went up to Jerusalem and got letters of authority and comes out of Jerusalem en route to Damascus to arrest God's servants. When he got out a piece from Jerusalem, the average preachers say "God knocked him off the beast." The Bible don't say that. The Bible says, "The light shined around about him, and he fell to the earth." It don't say he was knocked off the beast. Preach it like the Bible says— 9th Chapter Book of Acts. And Saul looked up and asked the question, "Who art thou, Lord?" And Jesus answered and said "I am Jesus whom thou persecutest; it is hard for thee to kick against the pricks." And then Saul asked him "What wilt thou have me to do?" That is a direct question, talking to Jesus face to face. Is there any one in this audience got nerve enough to say that God told him to "go in peace and sin no more, your sins are forgiven and soul set free?" Nobody got nerve enough to say that. Well, if you can't say it, what made you tell it? God hasn't told anybody that since Jesus died on Calvary. What did He tell Saul? Told him to go down to Damascus and it would be told him what he must do. Don't you know, and I know—you ought to know—that Jesus Christ can't save anybody independent of the preacher? He can't do it, He can't. Why folks, if he saves anybody independent of the preacher, He breaks His own law. His law says that a preacher must go and preach to the character, the preacher must tell the character what to do. If Jesus takes the job away from the preacher and does it Himself, He don't need a preacher; that fellow will have to get him another job. Don't you see you preachers have got it twisted? When Jesus commanded Ananias to go down and tell Saul what to do, what did he say? He says "he is praying now." Well, the sectarian people say that means praying for pardon. It doesn't mean any such thing. Why didn't Ananias tell Him "If he is praying, save him, just now I don't want to go down because I am afraid of him." I know he would have told him if God would have saved Saul without him. Ananias went down there after Jesus called him and said, "Brother Saul, why tarriest thou? Arise or get up and be baptized and wash your sins away, calling on the name of the Lord." I want to say just here that the baptism the Bible talks about and the one Ananias told Saul to submit to was for the purpose of washing away sins. And you all been saying that your sins was pardoned at the mourners' bench. There isn't a preacher in town can prove it. Brother Methodist and Brother Baptist, friends, get a sinner down here on the mourners' bench and they all circle around him, stay there all night trying to get him through. What do you want to get him through? If you don't mind, he will jump up and tell some excitable tale and that will be taken as evidence that he got it. My friends, Ananias just came to him, never told him to pray a bit. But stopped him, told him to get up and be baptized and wash his sins away. You know the average preacher in a protracted meeting—let me show you this: They call for mourners, how do they get them? "All Christians stand up." (Going to play a trick now.) Up jumps everything in the house, but two or three, and hardly a Christian in the house. Then after a while he says, "Sit down Christians, stand up sinners," and two or three sinners stand up. He plays a trick. "Come give me your hands," and the sinners walk down and give their hands. What is he trying to do? He says to them "sit down," and then they are considered mourners. Why not call for mourners and be through with it and not fool them? And if the sinners go back to their seats, they will burlesque him, "sit down there [on the mourners' bench] or you will be dead before this time next year." It's a shame, friends, a shame before God—the sinner will kneel down to keep from dying this time next year as the preacher told him. Preachers have done that right here in this town.

Well now, in conclusion, I want to ask tonight are there not some of you present that have never been baptized for the remission of your sins that would like to come to Jesus Christ just now with open hearts, hungering after the bread of life, with the determination to leave father, mother, husband and wife, losing sight of the world and say "I am coming to Jesus who shed his blood on Calvary that I might live?" I want to beg you in the name of Israel's God, will you not respond to the invitation tonight and believe the gospel of the Son of God?" Hebrews 11: 6, "Repent of your sins." Luke 13: 3, "Confess Jesus before men." Matthew 10: 32, "Buried with Christ in baptism for the remission of sins." Acts 2: 38, Romans 6: 4. Then you will become a member of the church we read about in the New Testament.

May God give you courage and may you have that love in your heart that will bring you to Jesus. "Come unto me all ye that labor and are heavy laden and I will give you rest. My yoke is easy and my burden is light." All taxation will be over. You need to come. Jesus said "today." Somebody says I have got plenty of time, but Jesus said "Today you hear my voice, harden not your hearts." Jesus says "Behold, I stand at the door and knock." He is knocking at the heart of every sinner that sits under this tent tonight. The invitation is extended, will you come?

WHO WILL BE ABLE TO STAND?

P.ing for pardon.

G—REligion.

Professing religion.

T.elling Ex.

V—OTing.

Saved.

Baptized because you are

    saved.

———————

SAND.

False Doctrine

Hear.

Believe.

Repent.

Confess.

Baptism.

New Life.

———————

Rock.

Christ.

CHAPTER VI.

___

"WHO WILL BE ABLE TO STAND?"

___

It is again that we come before you for the purpose of continuing the investigation of God's word as we have in the past services. We appreciate beyond words of expression this splendid audience at this time. It proves you are interested in your salvation. And another thing, it proves that the world has concluded that the gospel has not lost its prestige but when the gospel is preached in its purity and simplicity, that same respect and that reverence for God's word still exists in the hearts of men. So we appreciate very much the great manifestation of interest upon your part. That letter that Brother Miller has just read may not have appealed to you, but when you think of the great sacrifice that these white missionaries are making, endangering their lives that the native African may hear the gospel, it ought to make our hearts leap for joy. We ought to praise God for those bold and courageous missionaries that have gone out from the home land and have left loved ones and friends and gone into that country to spread the gospel of Christ, where they are likely to lose their own lives. And there is another side to the question and that is this: we must praise the Valdosta church of Christ, white, for their interest in and their coöperation with these missionaries and not only praise them, but all of the churches of Christ throughout the United States who are taking a great interest in these sacrificing Christian missionaries. And then I would like to call your

attention to a portion of that letter that states that
the native African is superstitious. We need not be
surprised at that. I guess our forefathers brought that
over here for we are yet superstitious. But, nevertheless, the point I make on that letter is that they are so
superstitious that the mother of the boy that wanted
to be baptized said if he was baptized, the whole family
would die. Poor thing! But that boy had so much
confidence in God and wanted to do what God said that
while Brother Brown, the Missionary, was baptizing a
few other natives, this boy, without the consent of his
mother, jumped in the river and while in the river, demanded baptism. He had more sense than we have on
this side. I don't know that I ever read of anybody on
this side jumping in the river to be baptized. I did have
an experience like this though at Decatur, Alabama. I
was baptizing one time in the Tennessee River and I
had six to baptize, as well as I can recollect, and when
I got out in the water, there were seven and I wondered where the seventh one came from and when I
got to him, he said "Brother Keeble, I haven't made
the confession yet." I said "Well, what are you doing
out here then?" He said "I thought you could take my
confession here as well as on the land." So I took his
confession and buried him beneath the waters of the
Tennessee River. That is almost like that boy in Africa.
That is an interesting letter and I appreciate it. It in-
spires me, though I am not in a foreign land, to work
harder in the home land, and to do my little bit, do
what little I can to bring others to Christ. We are glad
and very thankful that the gospel has such power that
it will bring men out of darkness into the marvelous light
of the Son of God. What is the matter with the people
of today? There can only be one conclusion and that is

they are not reading their Bibles. They are not searching the Scriptures. They put me in the mind of a nest
of mocking birds just hatched out. You that were
raised in the country know something about the nature
of mocking birds. They tell me when they are just
hatched out, they are blind and they can't see for nine
days and that puts upon the old mother the great re-
sponsibility of feeding them until they get large enough
and old enough to hunt food for themselves, and that
mother is just as busy as she can be going around
through the woods finding crickets, grasshoppers,
spiders and all kinds of insects as she may be able to
catch, and when she touches the leaves and makes a
little fuss, every little bird in the nest throws his mouth
wide open, and whatever that mother has, she deposits
it in the mouth of one of them and it closes in on it, not
knowing what it is. And so it is with the masses of the
people at large today, the preacher gets up and preaches.
He takes his text in the Bible and he leaves it pretty
soon and into the cemetery he goes. He preaches your
mothers', fathers' and all your dead kinfolks' funeral
and Oh! the shouting that takes place over that old
cemetery gospel. That's not found in the Bible. And
you have your mouth wide open sitting in the churches
like these birds, only you are blind spiritually and, like
the birds, you don't know what you are eating. You
ought to take time and examine what you are eating.
You are in a serious predicament. Had you been reading, you would have been in a Bible church. Had you
been reading, they never would have gotten you to the
mourners' bench. Had you been reading, you never
would have prayed for pardon. Had you been reading you
never would have got up and told that tale that Jesus told
you "Go in peace and sin no more." You made that

stuff up on account of not reading. Once more, the question is being circulated, "Why don't you use in-strumental music to help the service out?" You that have attended this meeting, give us justice; do we need any instrument? I think not. God knew what we needed—he didn't want you to use an instrument made by man, but to use that instrument He gave you. And we have used it tonight to His glory and to His honor.

While preaching at Jackson, Miss., a sanctified preacher, who represents the church that uses banjos, flutes, guitars, tambourines, horns, fiddles, and every-thing that he can get to make a fuss with, asked me why did we object to the use of instruments, and I told him if he could find where the Apostles, who were guided by the Holy Ghost, ever introduced or taught that an instrument was to be used in the church, we would use one. It isn't because we are so poor that we haven't an instrument, because you can buy anything now on installment, so we don't need to worry about an instrument, if we can get a dollar to pay down. I remember baptizing a man at Jacksonville, Florida, who belonged to the sanctified church. Brother Swanson was his name, a preacher; and he wanted an instru-ment to play in the church so bad and he didn't have the cash, so he went to a pawn shop to buy a guitar and deposited a dollar or so on the guitar, might have been over a dollar, but he deposited something and paid on it weekly, and at the time had it almost paid for. I went into that country preaching the gospel last year and he came to hear me. The first night he arose up in the tent, with a large crowd similar to this, and asked me some questions direct and I answered them and my answers made him mad. He left the tent almost run-ning and I thought I would never see him any more, but the very next night he was back there and walked up and made the confession. He had been reading all day and found out I was right, so he "cooled off." And if you people in Valdosta that are somewhat excited— not angry—if you will go home and read your Bible, you will cool off. So Swanson, after I baptized him, said to me "Brother Keeble, you know what I did? I went over to that pawnshop, after I obeyed the gospel, and told the pawnbroker I wouldn't need that thing and would he let me take that money up in something more profitable?" And the man consented, and he bought his wife some clothes, some things to wear that were more valuable than the guitar. And right tonight, you have got fine pianos and organs sitting in the church and the widows and orphans suffering. Hundreds of dollars wasted and the world hungry for bread. Something for somebody to bang on and a little selected crowd gathered around it and some sitting in the audience mad because they can't get around it too. That is right in your churches in Valdosta. And now friends, I am sorry that these things exist. I am sorry that any man will encourage anything in the church that will bring about discord. You ought not to do it. And again, when the choir is singing, the main part of the audience or congregation is sitting silent, and of course that makes them not in the worship at all. Only the choir in the worship and the rest are being entertained. Is that right? Entertainment is not service. Entertainment is not worship. Congregational worship is what God's word teaches. And then again, somebody said David used instruments and somebody says "Brother Keeble, what harm is it if David used it?" While at Fort Smith, Arkansas, two years ago, I told them that if David did use it, it was condemned. (Amos 6: 5.)

David took Uriah's wife—and you better not do like
him. Another point I wish to make concerning David.
He never was in the church of Christ, and you couldn't
take him for an example to run the church of Christ
by; he died before the church was established. And
another point that the religious world makes in favor
of instrumental music is, there is music in heaven. I
generally suggest that you had better wait until you
get there and then use it. I read in the Bible that
there are golden streets in heaven, but you don't walk
on them down here; you walk on them when you get
up there. You read also that there is a white horse in
heaven (Rev. 19: 11), but you don't ride him in the
church, so you can't prove instrumental music is right
because there is music in heaven. And another point
on instrumental music while I am on it. They say,
"What harm is it, Brother Keeble, to use the thing?
It don't hurt nothing." Let me ask you a question.
What harm is it to put cabbage and corn bread on the
Lord's table? What harm is it? Do you do it? No,
no harm in it, but we ought to eat corn bread and cabbage at home and you should play your instrument at
the same place. Thank God for his word, thank God
for the simplicity of His word and that simple New
Testament worship. No wonder God declares that His
people are a peculiar people, different to all others.
Don't work like no church in town. Nothing in town
works like the church of Christ. And now then, another
thought. While at Forth Smith, Arkansas, in a meeting in which there were eighty-six baptisms, there was
a lady and her husband that attended the meeting every
night and she would jot down on paper the passages
of Scripture that I would refer to and they would go
home and hunt for the passages, and while hunting one

night, she got stalled and she couldn't find a certain
passage, so she said to her husband, "It's almost two
o'clock in the morning, but I am going to call Brother
Keeble and ask him where is that passage of Scripture." So she called to the place where I was stopping and the lady of the house answered the phone.
The lady told her she would like to speak to Reverend
Keeble. People who don't know any better call me
"Reverend." Poor things don't know I never was a
Reverend and these folks that you are calling Reverend
around here never have been. That title never was
used but one time in the entire Bible (Psalm 111: 9),
and then it referred to God. No man is fit to be called
Reverend; no man, and yet we have got preachers that
will get fighting mad if you don't call them Reverend.
Have you ever read in the Bible about Reverend Doctor
Paul? No, and you have never read about Reverend
Doctor Peter. You have never read those titles in the
Bible and you never will. They had more respect for
God than to wear His title. Gentlemen, I pray the day
will come when that title will never be used in reference
to man, and our people be educated to the point whereby
that title and honor will only be used in reference to
God and not man. But back to the point. This woman
called up and the lady of the house came and knocked
on the door and said "Brother Keeble, it's very late,
but somebody wants to speak to you." The first thing
that jumped into my mind was, something is the matter at home. Any man that loves his family, when he
gets a long-distance call, gets nervous. He can't help
but think something is the matter at home. My mind
ran back to my home, and I told her "just as soon as I
can get dressed, I will go to the phone." I went and
picked up the receiver and said "Hello." The lady on

the other end said "Is that Brother Keeble?" and I said "Yes." She said "I want to ask you a question." Just as soon as I caught her voice, I knew it wasn't my wife and my nerves got quiet. So I said "What is it?" She says "Will you tell me where is that verse in the Bible that says Baptism washes away your sins?" I said "Acts 22: 16." Flop went the receiver. Poor thing was so glad to get it, she forgot to say "Thank you." And the next night she and her husband came walking down the aisle when the invitation was extended to make that confession that brought death to our Saviour and they demanded baptism to wash away their sins. Thank God for people that will sit up all night looking for a passage that says "Wash your sins away." I hope you will be that much interested tonight.

The subject tonight is "Who Will be Able to Stand?" That question tonight is of vast importance and I hope, as you listen to this lesson, that you will try to get the proper understanding and see whether or not you have built your house upon a rock and if you haven't then will you surrender and begin tonight to build your house upon the rock? Then you will be able to stand when my Jesus comes back. Over here on this side of the chart [pointing], we have at the bottom, sand. That means that everybody that do the things mentioned on this side is standing or building on sand. I don't care who it is. It is immaterial with me who does it. I can't take it back, neither can I fix it because you do it. Now then, this over here means that your house is built upon a rock. In the 7th chapter, Book of Matthew, Jesus Christ, the Lamb of God, says "Every one that heareth these sayings of mine, and doeth them not, shall be likened unto a foolish man, which built his house upon the sand. And the rain descended, and the floods came, and the winds blew, and beat upon that house, and it fell: and great was the fall of it." What made it fall? It was built on the sand. Now friends, for fear some of you don't understand, I will make this statement that the word "sand" in this text is figurative and has reference to the doctrine of man and not natural sand. But Jesus knew that the people that he was addressing would understand that no building that you want to stand is secure sitting on sand, because it is likely to be washed out from under him. Well, then friends, neither are you saved in any church today that don't preach or teach the Bible like the Apostles preached it. If you are in a church of that kind, your house is built upon the sand; the doctrine of men. In Matthew 15: 9, Jesus declared, "In vain they do worship me, teaching for doctrines the commandments of men." And in the same chapter he says: "If the blind lead the blind, both shall fall into the ditch." The blind leader is the man who preaches out of creeds and disciplines and thus governs the church. He is blind spiritually when he leads the people by creeds and disciplines and goes into Hitchcock's Manual. Somebody says, "Brother Keeble, what harm is there in disciplines?" I can tell you what harm there is in them. They make disciplines like they do automobiles, just as soon as one kinder plays out, there is another one made, and some of my old Methodist friends have got over a dozen disciplines. That old 1925 discipline is out of date and when the preacher tries that on the church, what do they tell him? "Parson, that is out of date, that ain't no account this year," and that shows you again that people are never satisfied, make their disciplines over and over and none of them suit them long. And Brother Baptist, he don't believe in disciplines, but he wants a manual; got a manual to see how to run the church and then he has to go down every year to the Association and squabble over the doctrine in the manual. I wouldn't belong to a church where God called me to preach and I couldn't preach until I see the big boys and let them fix me. Right now in your churches in this town, if God called a man to preach, he couldn't preach what God called him to preach without seeing the big boys and get them to fix him. Is that right? I dare you all to deny it; if you do, I will draw your manual and disciplines on you. Now listen, I met a man in Birmingham, Ala., and he said he had been called to preach for ten years. I said to him, "Are you not preaching?" "No Sir." "Well, what's the matter?" He said "I can't get them to ordain me." "Haven't you got a license?" He said "No, they won't give me any." My friends, just think of a man that is made to believe that he is called and can't preach until a set of men give him his license. We all ought to know that church is not right. Have to go to a set of men, after God called you from heaven and told you to go preach His word, and then you run up and ask the big boys "Please fix me." Then if you don't mind, they are going to make you pay for your license. They are all money machines, nothing but graft. There is nothing he can do to make you preach better than if he didn't lay his hands on you. Nothing he can do, but he makes you think so; he wants to get the money. And Brother Methodist, poor thing, after he gets his license and gets a permit to preach, can't go where he wants to go. he's got to wait until some man sends him somewhere. I met a Methodist preacher not long ago and I asked him "Are you coming back here next year?" He said "I'd like to mighty well, it's a good church, but I don't

know." Now there you are, he wants to come back
and don't know anything more than a little child. No
authority whatever, got to go and see what the big boys
say, and if he don't carry enough money, he'll have to
stand up before the conference and be burlesqued and
better not talk back to them, got to stand there and
take it. I pray God that the day will come when all will
learn that in the church that Jesus bought with His
blood there is privilege, there is liberty, there is freedom
in that church, and no set of men have any authority
over where you shall preach. You don't have to go up
every year to make a report, because God Almighty
made it free and told the preacher to go into all the
world, go where you please since you stay in the world.
Reckon you can stay in the world? Now then, Jesus
also said, "Whosoever heareth these sayings of mine, and
doeth them, I will liken him unto a wise man," that dug
deep and when he found the rock, he built his house
upon it; dig on through the disciplines, dig on through
the manuals—go on through and find you a rock, build
your house on nothing governed by disciplines, or manuals or any human creed. Dig on through these things
and find the rock, God's word. There is a rock down
there somewhere, dig on down. Christ said dig deep.
You've been here building on top of the earth. Dig
deep, my friends, you want your house to stand. Jesus
said that the man that builds his house upon a rock
will never fall, the rain may come and the wind may
blow, but his house will stand. Then listen, in Matthew
15th Chapter, 13th Verse, he said "Every plant, which
my heavenly Father hath not planted, shall be rooted
up." If you don't believe you'll be rooted up in these
other institutions or churches, you just stay there until

rooting time. Nobody won't get mad with you, just
stay there and you will regret it.

Now here [pointing] are the things that you have
done that puts you on the sand. The preachers taught
you these things. You've never taken time enough to dig
deep and find the rock, and when you woke up your
house was sitting flat on the sand. Now you are mad
because Brother Keeble is calling your attention to it.
You ought to be the happiest people in the world to
have your attention called to it. You ought to be happy
instead of getting mad. Go home and search your Bibles
—dig down and find you a rock to build your house on,
every bit of this doctrine of men is sandy. Teaching
sinners to pray for pardon is sandy. You have got
smart people in this town; before I came here, I heard
of the intelligence of this town. I was told that
there were some high-class educated people—I am not
flattering you. I believe it's true, that there are some
men in this town, educated, qualified preachers, and,
teachers, and of all professions in life who are in Valdosta, not one of them can find in the Bible where
God, through the Apostles, ever told any sinner to pray
for pardon. Tell them I said that. Nobody will bother
you. I am not afraid of anybody bothering that statement and if there is anybody in the audience that re-
members where any of the Apostles told any sinner to
pray for pardon, raise your hand and I will stop. Come
down the aisle and tell us where it is at in God's word
and I will ask forgiveness for the statement. I am
down here away from home and if I am in the dark
and I am begging for the light, and if you know the
light and won't bring it to me, God will damn you for
not telling where it is at in His word. All right, don't
let anybody tell you tomorrow that they could have

done it, because they can't. Make him tell you where it is; if it is in the Bible, your preacher should know where it is.

While preaching in Tuscumbia, Ala., a few years ago, a young girl fourteen years of age came to me one night and asked me for chapter and verse about "God heareth not sinners," and I gave it to her—John 9: 31. She went to her preacher the next day and asked him —I won't call his name, because he is dead—but he was pastor of that church for over 20 years. She went to the man and asked him—at the parsonage—whether sinners have to pray for pardon. He said "Child, what do you want to know that for?" She said "The man down here at the tent preached that last night and I want you to tell me where it is that sinners must pray for pardon so I can go down there and show it to him, because you have taught it to us and you should know where it is." He said "Child, the best thing you can do is to stay away from down there." Now isn't that pitiful? She didn't go up there to ask where she must go, she went up there to ask where the passage is that sinners must pray for pardon, and instead of having courage enough to say "It's not in the Bible." ashamed to acknowledge he was wrong, he tried to keep the little thing away from the meeting. Right now preachers are canvassing the town and telling you to stay away and they can't stay away themselves. Well now friends, build your house upon a rock, on the gospel of the Son of God, so it can stand until time shall be no more. The Bible does not teach sinners to pray for pardon. Another thing that is sandy is getting religion. Teaching men to get religion. Have you ever stopped to investigate that? Has anybody in the world got religion? If I say no, you will get mad, but I am

going to say no and you can get hot in the collar if
you want to. There's nobody in the world got religion
—I am spreading myself now—I remember my father-
in-law, S. W. Womack, said he was holding a meeting
once and stopping with a family who lived out in the
country. The old lady set a hen out in the hen house.
Her husband went out to the hen house and there was
eggs all around the hen so he raised the hen and counted
the eggs and there was about thirty-five. He went
back in the house and said "You are wasting those eggs,
too many under that hen." She said "Shut up and 'tend
to your own business, let her spread herself." You know
how the women tell us to attend to our own business.
She said "Let that hen spread herself." Now friends, I
said that to say this: When I tell you that there is not
a man in the world got religion, I am spreading myself.
The reason I know—I am not afraid or ashamed to say it
—is because religion is only mentioned in the Bible five
or six times and not a place says "get it." Let James
tell you what it is and you will learn you can't get it,
1st chapter 27th verse of James, "Pure religion and un-
defiled before God and the Father is this, To visit the
fatherless and widows in their affliction," not visit her
when she is well, but in her affliction. Men, your
trouble is visiting *well* widows. This Bible tells you
that the widow you visit must be *afflicted*. You ought
to know better. And He says, while visiting these
afflicted widows, to "keep yourself unspotted from the
world." It is a grave thing, religion. No need of you
hanging around these widows' houses every day and
they not afflicted. You ought to know better than that.
God told you to *do* religion, not *get* it; religion is a duty.
Religion is something that is practical and a man can't
get it. We are contending and are going to contend

until God takes us away from here that you can't get it. If you have got religion, will you please tell me where you got it and what does it look like? Why gentlemen, I have got a watch, don't amount to anything much, but if a man lost a watch in this town and the officers arrested and searched me tomorrow or tonight and say "This watch looks like the watch," I have got to tell where I got it. I stand there a perfect blank and can't tell where I got it. What does he do? He says "Come on and tell the Judge where you got it." I have to go up before the Judge and tell where I got the watch. And it is the same way with your religion; some day at the final consummation, you will have to tell the Judge about this religion you got down here. And friends, it's bad enough to claim you got religion, but it is still worse to jump up and profess it. I never heard any one profess religion in my life that didn't say too much. Tells something he don't believe and nobody else believes it. I will tell you of a man I once read of, he got religion and he got up and told the church he saw a big white horse and the horse had written on it, "Peace, peace," which let him know that he had made peace with his God. Peace on the horse and him running by! Well a woman is a funny thing, she generally knows when you make up something. And when he got home, this man's wife said "Look here, John, did you see anything, see a horse sure enough?" He kept on moaning, so happy. And she said "Just stop all that moaning and tell me." Oh! he was so happy over getting his religion. She said "John, stop that foolishness and tell me did you see any horse?" And he finally saw she meant business and he said "Why it looked like a horse." And when he said that, she said "You go back to the church and take back that lie." And you know a good many of you—I won't say lied—ought to go back and correct what you told. You never saw anything; you never heard nothing, but you told the church you did and you need to go back and fix it.

Then listen, there is a church that makes you tell your experience, then a set of men makes a motion, get a second and all in favor of accepting, let it be known by saying "I." A set of men testing God's work. Where did man get authority to vote on God's job? That set of men can vote and give you orders, right or wrong. That shows you that man puts himself above God. Every time he votes on a man that God fixed he puts himself above God, and instead of God being the final authority, he makes himself the supreme authority. If you have been voted on, you have been ruined. Then, any man that says he is saved before he is baptized contradicts God's word. You can't say that and prove it by the Bible that you are saved before you are baptized because the language found or the text used by Jesus after he had been taken off the cross, after he had been buried and after God Almighty at His own appointed time, raised Him from the dead, Jesus said: "All power is given unto me in heaven and in earth." (Matt. 28: 19.) "Go preach the gospel to every creature, he that believeth and is baptized shall be saved." (Mark 16: 15, 16.) If I ask this audience where saved comes in, you would say last, and that is correct. But if you had said saved and then baptized, that would be putting baptism last, when saved is last according to the word. You have got it twisted, you might as well walk up and fix it. No need of getting mad. I dare you to go home and read the Bible; if you do, I'll baptize you before Sunday. Read it and be honest and I'll baptize you before Sunday. This [point-ing] is sandy, teaching sinners to pray for pardon, get-ting religion, sandy; professing religion, sandy; telling experience, sandy; voting on candidate for baptism, sandy; saved before you are baptized, sandy; baptized because you are saved, sandy; that's all full of sand. There you are, I never fixed it, you did it. Now I want to ask you intelligent people one thing. I want chapter and verse for teaching sinners to pray for pardon. I want chapter and verse for getting religion. I want chapter and verse for professing religion; chapter and verse for telling your experience; chapter and verse for voting on candidate for baptism; chapter and verse for teach-ing sinners they are saved before baptism, and I want chapter and verse for baptism because you are saved. When you give chapter and verse, I will take out sand and put rock under this side of the chart. If you don't, I am going to let it stay a while.

All right, once more and I am through. On this side now [pointing]—"Where are you going, Keeble?" Going over to look for a rock. What you have to tell sinners to do is to hear the gospel. Mark 12: 29, Jesus said "The first of all the commandments is, Hear, O Israel; The Lord our God is one Lord." Next, believe 11th chapter Hebrews and 6th verse "But without faith it is impossible to please him; for he that cometh to God must believe that He is, and that He is a rewarder of them that diligently seek him." Right now, this audience have been taught that praying was seeking Jesus. You are mistaken. The word "prayer" means to petition or to ask for something. And the word "seek" means to look; different definition, different meaning, and you cannot make the two mean the same thing. In Isaiah 34: 16 it tells you to "Seek ye out of

the book of the Lord." Instead of you seeking out of
the book of the Lord, you go down to the mourners'
bench. Don't get mad because you did it. Get mad at
the man that had you go down, don't get mad at the
wrong man.

The next step is repentance—Luke 13: 3 Jesus Christ
says that "Except ye repent, ye shall all likewise perish." I told you all the other night that a man didn't
have to have a spasm to repent. He don't have to have
a fit to repent. He just decides, sitting out there or
wherever he hears the gospel and says "I am going to
quit bootlegging, I am through getting drunk, through
beating my wife, through bothering my neighbor's wife,
and I am through bothering my neighbor's husband,"
Then you have got to do it, when you repent you have
got to quit your devilment. While preaching this sermon at Fort Smith, Ark., an old woman popped up at
this point and said: "Keeble, if that's repentance, they
ain't nobody what's done it." Yes, a lot of folks claim
they've repented who have not quit their meanness;
but thank God some have repented, some have quit their
devilment. Yes, you got to quit. And another thing,
you are guilty of playing cards and many of you claim
to be Christians with two or three decks of cards in
your house right now. Some that claims to be Christians do not dance, but you are letting your children
dance in your home. Children dancing all over you and
you can't help yourself, and if the old man says anything about it, wife say "Let them children alone,
you'll run them away from home." I would stop it if
every one left. If you are going to dance in this house,
get out. Talk about running them off, let them go.
Another thing, supposed Christians today are doing
more worldly things than the real sinner. You can't

BAPTISMAL SCENE AT TAMPA, FLA.

hardly pass a Christian's home that you don't see them playing cards, dancing all hours of the night and go to church on Sunday, after dancing like a limber jack. My friends, it is time we were coming back to the truth and if you have repented, let those things alone, stop. Turn away from the world and tell the world I have quit. I have come out of the world and I am going to let my light shine. Repentance means, I will quit. Every man ought to be willing to quit. And after you repent, you must confess Christ. How is that confession made? With the mouth. Romans 10: "With the heart man believeth unto righteousness; and with the mouth confession is made unto salvation." Hearing is "unto"; repentance is "unto"; belief is "unto"; confession is "unto." Where do you get into, Keeble? That's right, baptism is *"into"*; that is the only thing that will put you "into" Christ. Well, what is that? Galatians 3: 27: "For as many of you as have been baptized into Christ have put on Christ." Only way you can get into Christ, baptized into Christ, put him on. Romans 6: 4: "Therefore, we are buried with him by baptism into death; that like as Christ was raised up from the dead by the glory of the father, even so we also should walk in the newness of life."

My friends, I want to say in conclusion, that when a man hears the gospel, that's rock; when he believes the gospel, that's a rock; when he repents, that's a rock; when he confesses Christ, that's a rock; when he is baptized, his house is built on a rock. Can't miss it to save your life. That is sandy over here. I gave you chapter and verse and you can't get around it. Are there any of you that are almost persuaded, are there any of you tonight that have seen your error, seen your mistake and have got courage enough to walk out and face a frowning and criticizing world? Stand up in the presence of this intelligent audience and confess with your mouth, confess what your heart believes? Jesus Christ, the Lamb of God who died on Calvary; that same Christ that God Almighty raised from the dead, after an angel from heaven rolled back the stone. This Lamb of God got up and declared that "all power in the heavens and in the earth is given unto me." That same Christ that raised Lazarus from the dead told you "Except a man be born of water and of the Spirit he cannot enter into the kingdom of God." (John 3: 5.) Are there any of you that has courage enough to start in and say "Brother Keeble, I see it, I am not ashamed. I tender myself?" Jesus said "If any man will come after me, let him deny himself and take up his cross and follow me."

We are going to grant you the privilege to come.

Printed in the United States
94844LV00006B/234/A

9 780892 255023